SRA
LANGUAGE CENTERS
for
YOUNG LEARNERS

aligned with
Language for Learning

 McGraw Hill SRA

Columbus, OH

Acknowledgement:

The publisher would like to thank Paula Bleakley for her help in preparing *Language Centers for Young Learners.*

SRAonline.com

The McGraw-Hill Companies

Table of Contents

Circle Time
Transitions
Center Activities
Books for Shared Reading

Activities

I. Introduction

Language Centers for Young Learners consists of 150 Center Activities that correlate with the lessons in *Language for Learning* and *Español to English* for Pre-K and Kindergarten classrooms. The activities in this guide reinforce the skills and concepts taught in *Language for Learning.* Along with the ideas for Center Activities, you will find Circle Time suggestions, ideas for Transitions, and Books for Shared Reading which lists trade books to use with your children. These ideas, suggestions, and books are designed to give children additional opportunities to learn the language of the classroom and to further develop oral language skills throughout the school day. All children need these additional opportunities, but they will be especially helpful for children who speak little or no English.

II. Scheduling *Language for Learning* Instruction and Daily Activities in Pre-K and Kindergarten Classrooms

In order for the *Language for Learning* program to accelerate and enhance student performance, each student must receive *Language for Learning* instruction every school day. Instruction time should be at least fifteen minutes in length from the beginning of the year. All preschool children should begin the program at lesson 1. If children's attention tends to wander, you may at first need to schedule two or three shorter sessions of *Language for Learning* instruction. Gradually extend the amount of instructional time based on children's ability to attend. If children do not complete an entire lesson one day, complete the lesson the next day. It is important the lessons be fun and engaging. (See the *Language for Learning* Teacher's Guide for additional information on adjusting the program for preschool children.)

You will need to develop a schedule to meet the specific needs of your school. External factors, such as school-assigned outdoor time, lunch time, and physical education instruction, must be taken into consideration and accommodated within the schedule.

The Group Activity (shown on the sample schedules) may consist of whole- or small-group activity when children work on pre-reading skills, such as phonemic awareness, letter names and letter sounds, or math skills.

Sample Full-Day Schedule—3 Groups

8:00 – 8:20	**Morning Circle**	(Circle 1)
8:20 – 9:00	*Language for Learning* **Instruction**	(Group 1)
	Center Activities	(Groups 2 and 3)
9:00 – 9:40	**Group Activity**	
9:40 – 10:10	**Outdoor Play**	
10:10 – 10:30	**Circle 2**	
10:30 – 10:50	**Music/Movement**	
10:50 – 11:30	*Language for Learning* **Instruction**	(Group 2)
	Center Activities	(Groups 1 and 3)
11:30 – 12:15	**Lunch**	
12:15 – 1:30	**Rest**	
1:30 – 1:45	**Circle 3**	
1:45 – 2:20	*Language for Learning* **Instruction**	(Group 3)
	Center Activities	(Groups 1 and 2)
2:20 – 2:45	**Outdoor Play**	
2:45 – 3:00	**Closing Circle**	

Sample Half-Day Schedule— 2 Groups

8:00 – 8:20	**Morning Circle**	(Circle 1)
8:20 – 9:00	*Language for Learning* **Instruction**	(Group 1)
	Center Activities	(Group 2)
9:00 – 9:40	**Group Activity**	
9:40 – 10:00	**Outdoor Play**	
10:00 – 10:15	**Circle 2**	
10:15 – 10:25	**Music/Movement**	
10:25 – 11:15	*Language for Learning* **Instruction**	(Group 2)
	Center Activities	(Group 1)
11:15 – 11:30	**Closing Circle**	

III. Suggestions for Arranging the Classroom

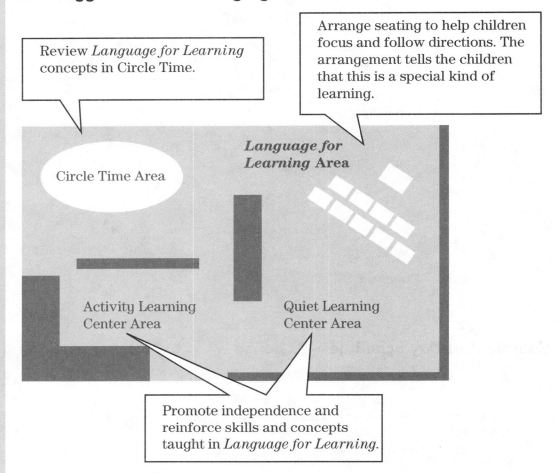

Review *Language for Learning* concepts in Circle Time.

Arrange seating to help children focus and follow directions. The arrangement tells the children that this is a special kind of learning.

Circle Time Area

Language for Learning Area

Activity Learning Center Area

Quiet Learning Center Area

Promote independence and reinforce skills and concepts taught in *Language for Learning*.

- Consider the physical layout. The room should be divided into active and quiet areas. Noisy centers, such as Housekeeping, should be kept away from quiet centers, such as Writing. Arrange materials within children's reach and provide storage space for center materials.

- Provide a safe environment. Make sure you can quickly see every nook and cranny of every area, even when teaching the *Language for Learning* lesson.

- Provide a variety of activities and materials. Materials should be concrete and manipulative. Activities and materials should allow children to make choices and should meet varied levels of ability.

- Introduce the centers to children each morning. Establish and explain the ground rules of each center.

- Open only two or three new centers or activities at a time and explain the purpose of each to the children. Keep in mind that some learning centers are appropriate for an entire week while you may want to make others available for only a day or two.

IV. Using Language Centers for Young Learners throughout the Day

Circle Time: Generally, a beginning circle time allows you and the children to get organized. For example, the Circle Time ideas in this guide suggest ways to help children learn the names of their classmates. Circle Time also assures that each child is welcomed daily and has an opportunity to participate in the morning activities. Each Circle Time activity reinforces a concept that has been taught during the actual *Language for Learning* instructional time. The closing circle helps children recap their day. Other circle times are for whole-group activities such as singing, poems, and stories.

Transitions: Transitions consists of Let's Focus and On the Move. When children need to be brought back on task, need a quick break, or are waiting in line, use one of the Let's Focus suggestions. Make these fun and fast-paced. Use On the Move suggestions to help move children from one activity to another or to line up in preparation for leaving the room.

Center Activities: Center Activities give children the opportunity to learn through active exploration and play. These are the suggested centers:

Art	**Motor**
Dramatic Play	**Painting**
Games	**Science**
Housekeeping	**Social Studies**
Listening/Speaking	**Sorting**
Math	**Writing**

Each activity is listed for use in one of these centers. However, most activities can fit in more than one center. For example, the Center Activity *Opposites—Big/Small* in lessons 91–100 is found in the Motor Center.

However, because it involves *sorting* of *seeds*, it could also have been listed as an activity in the Sorting Center or the Science Center. The activities may be used in any center you find most convenient for your classroom. Remember that the purpose of these activities is to give children the opportunity to review the concepts taught in *Language for Learning*.

Books for Shared Reading: Ten trade books are listed in Language Centers for Young Learners for each ten-lesson segment. The books were selected because of their relation to the concepts taught in the *Language for Learning* program. You will find books about concepts such as colors, opposites, occupations, and locations. These books offer another way for children to develop the background knowledge and vocabulary skills necessary to become good readers.

CIRCLE TIME

Polly, Put the Kettle On—Information—Names
(Teach the rhyme "Polly, put the kettle on; Sam, take it off again."
As you go around the circle, point to individual children using each child's name
as you and the children say:) *(Name), put the kettle on; (Name), take it off
again.*

If You're Happy—Actions—Body Parts
(Sing "If You're Happy and You Know It," substituting these words and actions:)
Stand up. (lesson 1)
Sit down. (lesson 1)
Touch your head. (lesson 4)
Touch your nose. (lesson 4)
Touch your hand. (lesson 5)
Touch your arm. (lesson 9)
Touch your ear. (lesson 10)

What's in the Bag?—Object Identification and Identity Statements
(Place common objects or pictures of the objects from lessons 1 through 10 in a
bag. Pull out one picture at a time. Have children identify the picture, using the
format from Identity Statements.)

Roll On—Object Identification
(Large cubes are available commercially, or use BLM 10 from Language Activity
Masters Book 1. In the pockets on each side of the cube, place pictures of
common objects learned in lessons 1 through 10. Children take turns rolling
the cube to one another and identifying the object that falls faceup. Encourage
children to "say the whole thing.")

Touch around the Room—Common Objects
(Using a pointer, review the common objects in the classroom: whiteboard,
door, window [lesson 7], flag, desk [lesson 9], cabinet [lesson 10]. As children's
responses become firm, have them take turns being the teacher and using the
pointer.)

TRANSITIONS

On the Move!
(Use the following activity as an effective way to transition from one activity to another.)

Let's Move—Information—Names
When I point to you, stand up.
Everybody, say his/her first name.
Good. _____, line up.

Let's Focus!
(Use the following activities as an effective break when children get restless.)

Simon Says—Actions
(Play Simon says, using the Actions format from lessons 1 through 10.)

Let's Break—Actions—Following Directions
Everybody, stand up. (Signal.) What are you doing? (Signal.) *Standing up.*
Everybody, sit down. (Signal.) What are you doing? (Signal.) *Sitting down.*

CENTER ACTIVITIES

✂ *Art*

What I Know Mural—Object Identification

Tape a piece of freezer paper to the wall or floor. Have children draw pictures of objects they can name. As they are working, ask them about the objects, using the language of the Object Identification and Identity Statements formats.

Dramatic Play

The Children on the Bus—Information—Names

Draw a large bus on freezer paper with windows for each child in the class. Put a photo of a child in each window. Using the Information—Names format, point to each child, and say, Everybody, what's his/her name?

Dramatic Play

Puppet Play—Action—Statements

Pair the children, and give each pair a puppet. One child in each pair can operate the puppet, giving the directions while the other child follows the directions. Example: *Touch your head (nose, hand, arm, ear).*

Dramatic Play

Action Tapes

Record five or six simple actions, using the language of the Actions—Statements format. Record new actions as you progress through the lessons. You could also place this tape at the puppet center. Children could play it and make puppets do the actions.

Games

Concentration—Object Identification

Play concentration with pairs of matching cards from the Picture Cards or with pictures from Language Activity Masters Book 1, BLM 5. At first, keep the cards faceup. The child chooses a card, names the object, and finds its match. As children progress, turn cards facedown, and play concentration.

Housekeeping

Pack a Suitcase—Object Identification

Place a small suitcase in the Housekeeping Center. Provide a variety of items for the center—clothing, small plastic bottles, jars, and containers, and so on. Have children pack the suitcase. Encourage them to tell each other what they're packing. Help them move from naming the object to saying the whole thing.

Materials: Freezer paper, crayons or markers

Materials: Freezer paper, photo of each child

Materials: Puppets

Materials: Recording of simple actions

Materials: Pairs of matching cards

Materials: Small suitcase, travel-sized plastic bottles and containers, clothing items

Materials:
Reusable
adhesive, rigid
foam, golf tees,
toy hammers

⚙ *Fine Motor*
Pegboard Match—Matching

Use reusable adhesive to attach a thick block of rigid foam to a table. Have a pile of colored golf tees and a hammer or two. Let children make matching pairs. Encourage children to tell about their matches.

Materials:
Laminated
pictures

⚙ *Fine Motor*
Puzzles—Matching Magazine Pictures

To prepare for future Part/Whole exercises, laminate some large, interesting pictures from magazines or old calendars. Cut the pictures in half. Put them in an activity center for children to match and to identify the pictures.

Materials: Paint-
stirring sticks,
paint, paint cans,
colored paper

○ *Sorting*
Stir It Up—Matching and Colors

To reinforce workbook matching exercises and color recognition, gather paint-stirring sticks from local paint stores. Paint the end of each stick a different color. (If you have enough sticks, paint several sticks of each color.) Store all the sticks in a paint can or another appropriately sized container. For each color used, wrap a matching color of paper around a can. Encourage children to match colors by putting each stick in the appropriate can.

Materials:
Finger paint,
large sealable
plastic bags,
whiteboards,
markers

✎ *Writing*
Colorful Cross-Out Mark Practice

Put a different color of finger paint into several large sealable plastic bags. Close the bags, and spread out the paint in each of the bags. Children use their fingers to practice making cross-out marks. To erase, children rub their hands over the bags, and the bags are ready to use again. Children may also use whiteboards and markers to practice making cross-out marks.

BOOKS FOR SHARED READING

If You're Happy and You Know It! by Jan Ormerod

Brown Bear, Brown Bear, What Do You See? by Bill Martin Jr

I Like Me! by Nancy Carlson

Wheels on the Bus by Raffi

School Bus by Donald Crews

Hop, Skip, Jump by Nicola Tuxworth

Blue Hat, Green Hat by Sandra Boynton

Freight Train by Donald Crews

Teddy Bear, Teddy Bear: A Classic Action Rhyme by Michael Hague

Who Is Tapping at My Window? by A. G. Deming

CIRCLE TIME

Fooler Game—Yes-and-No Questions and Identity Statements
(Teacher shows a common object, such as a ball, and follows the format for
Identity Statements:)
See if I can fool you with some hard questions!
Is this a boy? *No.*
Is this a tree? *No.*
Is this a ball? *Yes.*

Hickety, Pickety—Information—Names
(Teach the rhyme "Hickety, Pickety Bumblebee:")
Hickety, pickety bumblebee;
Who can say their name for me?
(Point to a student. She says her name.) *Pam.*
Let's all say it. Pam.
Let's all shout it. Pam.
Let's all whisper it. Pam.
Let's just clap it. (Clap the number of syllables in the name.)

Pass the Hat—Common Objects
(Play Pass the Hat. Put small common objects in a hat. Play music, and as the
music plays, children pass the hat. When the teacher stops the music, the child
with the hat reaches in, pulls out an object, and names it, using the Identity
Statements format *This is a _____.*)

Roll the Ball—Information—Names
(Children sit in a circle and greet each other by rolling a ball. One child says
Good morning, _____, and rolls the ball to that child. Continue until all children
have been greeted.)

Teddy Bear—Actions
(Teach the classic rhyme "Teddy Bear, Teddy Bear." Children follow along and do
actions they have learned in class.)

TRANSITIONS

(Use the following activities as an effective way to transition from one activity to another.)

On the Move!
Let's Leave—First, Next
First, we will line up. Next, we will walk to lunch. What will we do first? *Line up.* What will we do next? *Walk to lunch.*

Let's Move—Names
(Prepare two sets of name cards. Keep one set, and give each child his or her name card from the second set. Hold up a name card, and sing the following to the tune of "Where Is Thumbkin?")
Where is (name)? Where is (name)? (Child stands, holds up his or her name card, and sings:) *Here I am. Here I am.* (Then you sing:) (Name), how are you? We are glad to see you. Run away, run away! (Child gives the teacher his or her name card and "runs" away.)

Let's Focus!
(Use the following activity as an effective break when children get restless.)

Good Listening—Actions—Body Parts
Everybody, stand up. What are you doing? *Standing up.*
Everybody, sit down. What are you doing? *Sitting down.*
Everybody, put on your listening ears. (Children mime putting on listening ears as in putting on headphones.)

CENTER ACTIVITIES

Materials: Picture cards showing actions

Dramatic Play

Actions

In a small group or in pairs, have children choose an action card from the Picture Cards. Direct them *not* to show it to anyone. Children take turns acting out their card for the group. The group tells what the child is doing. Examples: *You are jumping. You are eating.*

Materials: Play foods, kitchen utensils

Housekeeping

Foods—Identity Statements

In a kitchen center, provide a variety of play foods to "cook" with. As children are cooking, ask them about the foods they are making. Have them "say the whole thing."

Materials: Photos of each child

Listening/Speaking

Name Game—Information—Names

Take a photo of each child. Hold up each photo, and using the format of "Brown Bear, Brown Bear," repeat with children: *(Shawnee, Shawnee), who do you see?* Hold up the next photo, and say with children: *I see (Pam) looking at me!* Continue until each child's photo has been shown. Pictures can be mounted on paper and stapled together to create a class picture book. Create a cover, and add a title. Example: "Who's in Our Class?"

Motor

People Patterns—Actions

Invite three or four children to be part of a pattern. Ask one child to stand and the next to sit. Ask the other children to "read the pattern." One by one, add children to the pattern. When all are part of the pattern, children can name the pattern by saying their placement *(standing, sitting)* as you point to each child down the line. Invite children to make a new pattern.

Materials: Card stock, magnetic tape, pictures of objects, dowels, string, magnets

Fine Motor

Fishing for Objects—Common Objects/Identity Statements

Cut out pictures of common objects from magazines. Glue pictures to card stock and attach a piece of magnetic tape to each picture. Make simple fishing poles from dowels and string, attaching a magnet to the end of the string. Children "fish" for a picture. When a "fish" is caught, they identify the object and "say the whole thing."

Motor

Music and Movement—Basic Information

Cut out simple shapes of a child, a teacher, and a school. The shapes should be large enough for a child to stand on. Tape the shapes to the floor. Have children stand and make a circle. Select one child to stand on each shape. Start the music. ("Mr. Al's Back-to-School Bop" is a good song for this activity.) Children walk around in a circle as the music is playing. When you stop the music, children stop moving. Ask each child who lands on a shape the question for *name, teacher,* or *school*. Follow the Information format.

 Science

Silhouettes/Shadows—Actions

Project a bright light onto a wall. Encourage children to position his or her hands, arm, or head between the light and the wall. Ask children: Touch your head. What are you doing? *Touching my head.* Touch your nose. What are you doing? *Touching my nose.* Children enjoy seeing the shadow of the action they made with their body.

 Sorting

Shoe Sort—Matching

Teach the rhyme "We have shoes, in sets of two. Come on in, and see what's new!" Hang a shoe bag in the center. Give children a basket of shoes. Children match the shoes and put the pairs in the shoe bag. This works for sorting socks into pairs also.

 *Sorting*

Oh Nuts!

To support future classification exercises, place a pair of tongs in a basket filled with two kinds of unshelled nuts. Children use the tongs to sort the nuts into two piles.

 Writing

Whiteboard Drawing—Object Identification

Provide individual whiteboards and markers. Have children draw objects they can name. As they are working, ask them about the objects, using the language of the Identity Statements and Object Identification tracks.

Materials: Shapes of a child, a teacher, and a school; masking tape; recording of "Mr. Al's Back to School Bop" or other music

Materials: Projector

Materials: Shoe bag, basket of shoes

Materials: Two kinds of unshelled nuts, tongs

Materials: Whiteboards, markers

BOOKS FOR SHARED READING

Brown Bear, Brown Bear, What Do You See? by Bill Martin Jr

The Animal Boogie by Debbie Harter

From Head to Toe by Eric Carle

Clap Your Hands by Lorinda Bryan Cauley

Chrysanthemum by Kevin Henkes

The Old Woman Who Named Things by Cynthia Rylant and Kathryn Brown

Yellow Ball by Molly Bang

Have You Seen My Cat? by Eric Carle

Who Is Tapping at My Window? by A. G. Deming

Growing Colors by Bruce McMillan

My Name Is Yoon by Helen Recorvitis

Teddy Bear, Teddy Bear: A Classic Action Rhyme by Michael Hague

CIRCLE TIME

Good Morning—Information—Names

(Children sit in a circle. Teacher starts the greeting by turning to child on his or her right, shaking hands, and saying:) Good morning, (Name).
(Children continue the greeting around the circle, shaking hands and saying:
Good morning, (Name).

Who Stole the Cookie—Information—Names

(Teach children the chant "Who Stole the Cookies from the Cookie Jar?"
Teacher begins:) (Name) stole the cookies from the cookie jar. *Who me?*
Yes, you! *Couldn't be.* Then who?
(The chant begins again with the child who was "it," choosing the name of the next child. Continue around the circle until every child has had a turn to be "it.")

Hop to It—Actions—Colors (Yellow, Red, Blue)

(Cut out several lily pads in different colors.)
(Name), hop to the (color) lily pad.
(Child named hops to the lily pad, names the color, and hops back.)

I See My—Part/Whole—Head

(Children sit in a circle and pass a mirror. A child looks in the mirror and says, *I see my [name part of head].* The child passes the mirror to the next child, who repeats the sentence naming a part of his or her head. Continue until all children have had a turn.)

TRANSITIONS

On the Move!
(Use the following activities as an effective way to transition from one activity to another.)

Line Up—First, Next—Names
(Call on students, using *first, next:*)
First, (name) lines up. Next, (name) lines up.

I Spy—Changing Activities—Lining Up
I spy children wearing blue. (Children wearing blue choose a center.)
I spy someone wearing red shoes. (Child goes to a center.)

Let's Focus!
(Use the following activity as an effective break when children get restless.)

Yes-or-No—Actions
(Anytime children need some movement or need to refocus their attention, follow the Actions format with yes-or-no questions:) Everybody, touch your head. (Children touch their heads.) What are you doing? *Touching my head.* Are you touching your head? *Yes.* Are you touching your leg? *No.*

CENTER ACTIVITIES

Housekeeping

Missing Objects—Object Identification

Provide a basket with small common objects from your Housekeeping Center and a tray. Children watch as you place three objects from the basket on the tray. Children shut their eyes. Remove one object. Children open their eyes and tell what object is missing. As children understand how to play, let them take turns playing the part of the teacher.

Materials: Basket, tray, common objects

Listening/Speaking

Language Response

Read *Mice Squeak, We Speak* several times to children. Then record your reading with children making appropriate noise. Put in the Listening Center for children to enjoy. Provide paper and crayons, and encourage children to draw their favorite part of the story.

Materials: Mice Squeak, We Speak, recorder, drawing paper, crayons

Math

Patterns—Circles, Circles

Use masking or colored tape to make circles on a tabletop. Provide a variety of math counters. Have children create their own unique patterns along the circles. Ask children to describe their patterns to reinforce the shape name.

Materials: Colored tape, math counters

Fine Motor

Potato Head—Actions—Part/Whole (Body Parts)

Give each child a sweet potato and scraps of construction paper to build a head with the parts children have learned. Provide either eyes, noses, mouths, and ears made of construction paper, or have children tear or cut these out. Each child builds a head by gluing the parts on the sweet potato. As children build their heads, ask them to tell the parts they have used following the language of Part/Whole. *My potato head has eyes. My potato head has ears.* To incorporate some science in this activity, help children place four toothpicks around their potato, leaving about one-third of the potato below the toothpick. Fill a cup with water, and place the potato in the cup with the toothpicks holding it so the bottom one third of the potato is in the water. The potatoes will root and grow leaves (hair).

Materials: Sweet potatoes, construction paper, glue, toothpicks, plastic cups

Materials: Action photos of children, cube-shaped box, glue

Gross Motor
Roll It—Actions
Take six photographs of children doing different actions such as hopping, clapping, touching their heads, and so on. Glue one photo to each side of a cube-shaped box. In a small group or in pairs, children take turns rolling the cube. The child who rolled the cube performs the action shown. The child asks the rest of group, *What am I doing?* Children respond, *You are hopping.* If necessary, remind children to "say the whole thing." Play continues as the next child rolls the cube, performs the action, and asks the question.

Materials: Containers, funnels, rice, beans

Sensory/Motor
Pouring Rice/Beans—Opposites (Full/Not Full)
Have children fill the containers to various levels using the rice and beans. Point to each container, and ask children if the container is *full* or *not full.* Children also enjoy playing this game with each other.

Materials: Shoe organizer with clear pockets, basket, pairs of objects (see activity)

Science
Pockets—Matching
To reinforce matching and to prepare for future classification activities, hang a shoe organizer with clear pockets near the science table. Provide pairs of objects such as leaves, shells, nuts, flowers, fake bugs, and so on. Put one object from each pair in one of the pairs of pockets on the shoe organizer, leaving the matching pocket empty. Have the matching objects in a basket. Children place the matching objects in the empty pockets to complete each pair.

Materials: Magnet boards, magnets

Science
Magnet Fun—Prepositions—On and Over
Provide a small group of children with magnet boards or baking sheets. Give each child a collection of interesting magnets. Alternate asking children to place a magnet *on* the magnet board or to hold the magnet *over* the board.

Materials: Pictures of places in your town, poster board, markers, drawing paper

Social Studies
This Is My City—Information: City, Town
Take pictures of easily identified places around your town such as the grocery store, the post office, and the park. Make a poster with the photographs and the name of your town. Provide markers and paper. Have children pick one of the places on the poster and draw something they do at that place.

Materials:
Laminated coloring
book pages
showing objects
learned, dry-erase
markers, wipes

 *Writing*

Cross-Out/Circle

Laminate simple coloring book pages that show several objects children have learned. Provide dry-erase markers and wet wipes. Record short directions for children to follow: Cross out the dog. Circle the house.

BOOKS FOR SHARED READING

Mice Squeak, We Speak by Tomie dePaola

Jump, Frog, Jump by Robert Kalan

Go Away, Big Green Monster by Ed Emberley

Catalina Magdalena Hoopensteiner Wallendiner Hogan Logan Bogan Was Her Name by Tedd Arnold

If You Take a Mouse to School by Laura Numeroff

I Need a Lunchbox by Jeanette Caines

Mouse Paint by Ellen Stoll Walsh

Brown Rabbit's Shape Book by Alan Baker

What Color Is Your Underwear? by Sam Lloyd

The Color Kittens by Margaret Wise Brown

CIRCLE TIME

Charades—Actions—Pronouns
(Choose one topic that children are familiar with such as actions you can do on the playground. Encourage a child to act out a playground activity. Other children guess what he or she is doing. Encourage children to use the pronouns *you, he,* and *she.* Children respond:) *You are hopping. He is swinging. She is running.*

Which Room in the House—Common Objects—Classification/Critical Thinking
(To develop vocabulary and to prepare for future classification skills, gather common household objects from various rooms of a house. Place objects in a laundry basket. Hold up one object at a time, and ask:) What is this? (Children say the whole thing.) *This is a (name of object).* In which room of a house could you find this? (Answers will vary.)

What Is That?—First, Next
(Stand behind a door, an easel, or a room divider, and make two sounds or record pairs of sounds ahead of time. Examples: Tap your foot and then crunch paper; clap, and then ring a bell. Then ask:) Which sound did you hear first? (Children identify sound.) Which sound did you hear next? (Children identify sound.)

Silly Moves—Actions—Body Parts
(Follow the language of the Actions—Body Parts format:) Point to your nose. Point to your wrist. (Then shake it up with silly moves.) Touch your nose to your wrist. Point to your elbow. Point to your knee. Touch your elbow to your knee.

TRANSITIONS

On the Move!

Line Up—Hop like a Bunny—Actions

I'll name an action. You'll name an animal that moves this way. **Hop.** (Call on different children to name an animal that hops. If a child names an animal that hops, he or she hops to line up or to go to the next activity. Continue with different action words such as *swim, walk, fly.*)

Can You Name?—Colors

(Sing "London Bridge Is Falling Down," substituting these words:)
Can you name your favorite color?
Favorite color, favorite color?
Can you name your favorite color?
Tell us, (name). **(Name) says favorite color and goes to next activity.**

Let's Focus!

Beanbag Animals—Prepositions

(Use a favorite beanbag baby (frog) and a pretend bug or any other interesting object:) Everybody, is this bug *over* the frog? (Hold the bug over the frog.) *Yes.* Say the whole thing about where this bug is. *This bug is over the frog.* (Continue with *on* and *in front of.* Add the "not" statement after lesson 39.)

Pencil, Toothbrush—Part/Whole

(To get children focused in line and ready to go, hold up a pencil and review its parts. Say:) Get ready to tell me the parts of a pencil. Say the whole thing. (Touch the shaft.) *A pencil has a shaft.* (Continue with eraser and point.)

CENTER ACTIVITIES

Materials: Freezer paper, circle-shaped foods for snacks

Art
Circles, Circles—Shapes
Provide a large piece of freezer paper. Brainstorm with children to name a list of foods that are circle shaped. Encourage children to draw their favorite circle-shaped foods. When they are finished, have several circle-shaped foods to choose from for snack time.

Materials: Table, pencil, head, toothbrush, drawing paper, markers

Art
Part/Whole—Table, Pencil, Head, Toothbrush
Provide these objects for the children to look at. Using the language from the Part/Whole format, ask children to name the parts of each object. Provide drawing paper and markers, and invite children to draw themselves using the table, pencil, or toothbrush.

Materials: Play phones, pictures of your school, city, teacher

Dramatic Play
Information Please!—Information—School, City, Teacher
Provide several play phones and pictures of your school, city, and teacher. Encourage children to play in pairs, phoning for information. One child shows the picture of the school, talks into the phone, and asks his or her partner: *What is the name of your school?* Children continue with *city* and *teacher* and then switch roles.

Materials: Flannel or heavyweight fabric interfacing, hook-and-loop tape (to make flannel-board characters for stories from Storybook 1)

Dramatic Play
Flannel Board—Story Retelling
By lesson 40, children have heard several poems and stories from Storybook 1 in Presentation Book A. Class favorites are often the poem "My Cat, My Dog, My Frog" and the stories "Polly and the Lion," "Marvin the Eagle," and "Oscar the Worm." Make simple flannel-board characters from flannel, heavyweight fabric interfacing (can be colored with markers), or laminated pictures. Attach hook-and-loop tape to the backs. Have the flannel-board characters available for children to use in retelling their favorite stories.

Materials: Index cards, masking tape, celery sticks, peanut butter, raisins

Housekeeping
Little Cooks—First, Next, Last
In advance, plan a simple recipe involving three steps, such as celery sticks filled with peanut butter and topped with raisins. Use three index cards to illustrate each step. Using masking tape or colored tape, make an arrow on a table. Place the cards along the arrow so children can "follow" the recipe. Have plates or napkins and recipe ingredients available for children. As children follow the recipe, circulate and ask: What do you do first? *Get celery stick.* What do you do next? *Put on peanut butter.* What do you do last? *Put on raisins.*

Listening/Speaking

Overhead Fun—Review—Who, Doing What, Where

Make an overhead transparency of lesson 38, exercise 7. Provide wet-erase overhead projector markers. Children work in pairs. Place the transparency on the overhead projector. Record the review questions from the exercise, and add simple directions: Who is eating an apple? Cross out who is eating the apple. What is in the water? Cross out what is in the water. Continue with remaining review questions from the exercise. Later, instead of using the recording, have children work in pairs, taking turns asking review questions and making cross-out marks.

Materials: Transparency of lesson 38, exercise 7; recording (see activity); wet-erase markers

 Math

Sorting—Opposites

Provide several containers with water (baby food jars with lids on work well). Fill some jars all the way, and some part way. Add food coloring to the water for fun. Invite children to sort the jars as *full* and *not full.* Use a collection of sponges in various shapes such as numbers, letters, or animals. Provide a shallow pan of water, and encourage children to "wet" some sponges and leave some sponges "not wet." Ask children to sort sponges as *wet* and *not wet.* Provide a collection of leaves, shells, or counting manipulatives. Encourage children to sort the items as *big* or *not big.*

Materials: Containers, water, food coloring, sponges, counting manipulatives

 Fine Motor

Humpty Dumpty Puzzles—Names

Write each child's name on an egg-shaped piece of card stock. Decorate, or have children decorate, with glitter and stickers. Cut names in half, and put in sealable plastic bags. Place name bags in a center along with a chart listing children's names. Encourage children to put their own names and classmates' names back together again.

Materials: Card stock, glitter, stickers, sealable plastic bags

Fine Motor

Wax-Covered String Sticks/Play Dough—Names

Provide laminated name cards for each child. Have children use wax-covered string manipulatives or play dough to follow the letters on their cards to "write" their names.

Materials: Laminated name cards, wax-covered string or play dough

Materials: Dot markers, dot stickers, paper plates

 Writing

Circle Stories—Vocabulary Development

Invite children to decorate their paper plates using dot markers and stickers. When children are finished, ask them to describe their work. Write comments on their plates. Encourage children to share decorated plates and comments with classmates.

BOOKS FOR SHARED READING

Ten Black Dots by Donald Crews

Little Blue and Little Yellow by Leo Lionni

City Street by Douglas Florian

Good Morning, Good Night by Michael Grejniec

Push, Pull, Empty, Full: A Book of Opposites by Tana Hoban

Kitten Can . . . by Bruce McMillan

I Spy: An Alphabet in Art by Lucy Micklethwait

Yo! Yes? by Chris Raschk

It Looked Like Spilt Milk by Charles G. Shaw

What Am I? Looking through Shapes at Apples and Grapes by N.N. Charles

CIRCLE TIME

Action Statements—Pronouns/Colors

(Place the colors taught on the sides of a cube—red, yellow, blue, black. Roll the cube. Children wearing the color that appears faceup, stand up. Follow the format for Action/Pronouns using *you, I, he, she, we,* and *they.*) Everybody, what are *they* wearing? (Children say color name.) *Red.* Say the whole thing about what (*you, I, he, she, we,* or *they*) are wearing. *(They) are wearing (red).*

Beanbag Animals—Prepositions

(Place a chair so it is facing children. Review the prepositions *in front of, on,* and *over* by positioning a small stuffed animal (frog) and asking:) Where is the frog? *(Preposition) the chair.* (Ask for volunteers to place the frog *in front of, over,* or *on* the chair, and ask the rest of group:) *Where is the frog?* (Ask children to "say the whole thing.")

Pictures—Review

(Show children a large, interesting picture. Old calendar pages work well. Follow the format for Review exercises, asking questions using the words *what, which, on,* or *over.*)

Syllable Clap—Days of the Week

(Model, and then lead children as you say the days of the week, clapping the syllables. Children will soon get the pattern that all days have two claps except for Sat • ur • day.)

TRANSITIONS

On the Move!

Information—Names, School
(Call children to circle time by teaching this rhyme to the tune of "The More We Get Together:")
We're so glad you're in our classroom, our classroom, our classroom.
We're so glad you're in our classroom at (name of school).
We're glad to have (child's name) and (name) and (name).
We're so glad you're in our classroom at (name of school).
(Repeat until all children are at the circle.)

Let's Focus!

Movement—Opposites
Sit down (pause) and stand up.
Push (pause) and pull.
Move your fingers through the air fast (pause) and slow.
Shake your head yes (pause) and no.
Make a happy face (pause) and a sad face.

Follow the Leader—Actions
This is what I can do. (Demonstrate a movement such as stomping feet.)
Everybody, do it too! (Group copies leader's movement.)
This is what I can do. (Movement continues.)
Now, I'll pass it on to you. (Point to new leader who continues the rhyme using a different action.)

CENTER ACTIVITIES

✂ *Art*

Look in the Yellow Pages—Colors
Provide black construction paper and the yellow pages from an old telephone book. Have children tear or cut up the pages, and then glue them to black construction paper to make yellow-page collages.

✂ *Art*

Make a Tree—Part/Whole
Provide materials for making paper trees. Remind children that their trees should have trunks, roots, leaves, and branches. After children complete their trees, glue the trees to the freezer paper, and hang your classroom "forest."

 Dramatic Play

Flannel Board—Part/Whole
Provide simple flannel pieces of the parts of objects learned in the Part/Whole exercises—elephant, tree, wagon, pencil, toothbrush. (Or laminate Part/Whole pictures from the program, and cut these apart. Attach hook-and-loop tape on the back of each part.) Place the pieces of each object in separate resealable plastic bags. Children take a bag and place the pieces on the flannel board to make the whole object. Encourage children to use the language of Part/Whole as they place the pieces: *A tree has roots, a tree has leaves,* and so on.

🎮 *Games*

Build an Elephant—Part/Whole
Use BLM 45A and BLM 45B from the activity Build an Elephant in Language Activity Masters Book 1. Have children play this game in a small group or with a partner. Laminate one game board (BLM 45A). Laminate and cut out two or three copies of BLM 45B. Follow the directions for playing the game, but instead of gluing the elephant parts, children will simply place them next to the body to complete their elephant. The game board and parts can be stored and reused.

Concentration—Opposites
To reinforce *big* and *small*, make a simple matching game. On index cards, draw simple objects for children to match. For example, on one card, draw a big square; on a second card, draw a small square, and so on. Initially, play the game with cards faceup. As children become firm, turn cards facedown, and children play concentration.

Materials: Yellow pages from telephone book, black construction paper, glue

Materials: Freezer paper, construction paper, scissors, markers, crayons, yarn, glue

Materials: Flannel or laminated pictures of the parts of objects from Part/Whole exercises, resealable plastic bags, hook-and-loop tape

Materials: One laminated copy of BLM 45A, two or three laminated copies of BLM 45B from Language Activity Masters Book 1, game markers (colored buttons)

Materials: Index cards (see activity)

Listening/Speaking

Listen for Colors

After listening to the recording of *Is It Red? Is It Yellow? Is It Blue?*, provide children with drawing paper and red, yellow, and blue crayons. Have children draw their favorite part of the story. Encourage children to share their drawings with the class.

Materials: Recording of the story *Is It Red? Is It Yellow? Is It Blue?* by Tana Hoban, drawing paper, crayons (red, yellow, and blue)

Motor

Actions—First, Next

Use the Picture Cards that show actions, or take your own photos of people doing actions children have learned. Tape an arrow on the floor or table top. Playing with a partner, one child chooses two action pictures and places them on the arrow. He or she then does the actions and asks the partner: *Tell me what I did first; tell me what I did next.*

Materials: Picture Cards showing actions, masking tape

Fine Motor

Cereal Fun—Pair Relations

Draw a line down the middle of several index cards. Glue one piece of cereal to each half of the index card. Make five or six different pair combinations—moon/star and so on. Place these cards so children can easily see them. Provide index cards with the line drawn down the middle and a bowl of cereal. Children choose an "empty" index card and place cereal on it to match a teacher-made card. Encourage children to describe their pairs. *First, there's a moon; next, there's a star.* When children are finished making pairs, they may eat the cereal.

Materials: Breakfast cereal that contains various shapes, index cards, glue

Science

Classifying Leaves—Sorting

Point out that tree leaves come in many shapes and sizes. Ask children to collect different types of tree leaves. Divide children into small groups, and give each group a variety of leaves. Encourage children to sort their leaves by similar attributes such as shape, color, size, and so on. Have them glue samples to a large sheet of paper. Encourage each small group to share their "sorts" with the rest of the class.

Materials: A variety of leaves children have collected, large sheet of paper for each small group, glue

Materials: Two resealable plastic bags, pictures of objects that show opposites (see activity)

● *Sorting*

Sorting—Opposites

In one resealable plastic bag, place pictures showing objects that are *wet* or *dry*. In the other bag, place pictures showing objects that are *big* or *small*. Invite children to sort pictures: *wet, dry; big, small.* Ask children to name other object pairs that are *big* or *small, wet* or *dry*.

BOOKS FOR SHARED READING

Have You Seen Trees? by Joanne Oppenheim

The Tremendous Tree Book by May Garelick and Barbara Brenner

Is It Red? Is It Yellow? Is It Blue? by Tana Hoban

Red Leaf, Yellow Leaf by Lois Ehlert

Opposites by Mary Novick and Sybel Harlin

Blueberries for Sal by Robert McCloskey

Mary Wore Her Red Dress and Henry Wore His Green Sneakers by Merle Peek

Hide and Seek in the Yellow House by Agatha Rose

Chocolate Chip Cookies by Karen Wagner

Who Is the Beast? by Keith Baker

CIRCLE TIME

Stand, Squat, Sit—Top, Middle, Bottom
(Make a simple traffic light from poster board. Move a clothespin from red to yellow to green as you review *top, middle,* and *bottom* with children:)
Now let's play a game. When the clothespin is on red at the *top,* you stand up and stretch your arms up. (Model action for children.) When the clothespin is on yellow in the *middle,* you squat. (Model action for children.) When the clothespin is on green at the *bottom,* you sit. (Model action for children. When children's responses are firm, have a child be the teacher and move the clothespin.)

Fish in Bowl—Actions/Tense
(Using a stuffed-animal fish and an empty fish bowl, follow the format for Actions/Tense. Place fish in bowl, and say:) Everybody, where is the fish. *In the bowl.*
Say the whole thing. *The fish is in the bowl.*
(Hold fish over the bowl.) Where is the fish? *Over the bowl.*
Say the whole thing. *The fish is over the bowl.*
Listen, where was the fish before it was over the bowl? *In the bowl.*
Say the whole thing about where the fish was before it was over the bowl. *The fish was in the bowl.*
(Repeat the activity using other prepositions—*on, in front of, in back of.*)

Did You Ever See a Fishy?—Opposites
(Give each child a paper fish. Designate a pair of opposite movements, such as *over* and *under,* each time you sing the song below, and encourage your "school of fish" to swim this way and that. Sing the following to the tune of "Did You Ever See a Lassie?")
Did you ever see a fishy, a fishy, a fishy,
Did you ever see a fishy swim this way and that?
Swim this way and that way, and that way and this way;
Did you ever see a fishy, swim this way and that?
(Substitute other word pairs such as *up/down, high/low, in front of/in back of.*)

Who's Missing?
(Ask a volunteer to close his or her eyes. Ask a second volunteer to hide where he or she can't be seen. Ask the first child to open his or her eyes and look at the remaining children in the group. Provide the child with plenty of chances to guess the name of the child who is hiding. Continue to play as a new volunteer hides.)

Calling All Cows—Plurals
(See Calling All Cows in Center Activities.)

TRANSITIONS

On the Move!

Big Fish Bowl—Empty/Full and Colors
(To move children from one activity to another, give each child a die-cut fish in one of these colors: blue, black, green, red, yellow. Provide a glass fish bowl, and sing the following to the tune of "The Muffin Man.")
Look and see my big fish bowl,
My big fish bowl, my big fish bowl.
Look and see my big fish bowl,
As empty as can be!
Now I put a (color) fish in,
(Color) fish in, (color) fish in.
Now I put a (color) fish into my big fish bowl.
(As their fish color is called, children come up, drop their fish in the bowl, and go to designated activity.)

Let's Focus!

Plurals
(To focus attention once children are lined up, use the language of the Plurals format.) Am I holding up finger or fingersssss? (Repeat several times. Have children perform actions.) Touch your ear. (Pause.) Touch your earssss. (Pause.)

Classification Game
(Ask a question, and see how many different answers children can give. Some examples are as follows:) What are some things that fly? What do you like on pizza? What do you eat for breakfast?

CENTER ACTIVITIES

✂ *Art*
Shiny Rainbow Fish—Circles

Provide a simple fish cutout as well as circles cut from colored paper and aluminum foil to use for scales. Encourage children to decorate their fish with the circles. Children may enjoy using their fish to play the circle game Did You Ever See a Fishy?

Materials: Craft sticks, crayons, scissors, glue, drinking straws, tape

✂ *Art*
Short-to-Long Doggie: Opposites—Short/Long

Provide one copy of BLM 55 from Language Activity Masters Book 1, two craft sticks, crayons, scissors, glue, one drinking straw, and tape for each child. Follow the directions on page 29 of Language Activity Masters Book 1. When dogs are completed, ask children: Show me a short dog. Show me a long dog.

Materials: Paper plates, die-cut cows, glue

☎ *Listening/Speaking*
Calling All Cows—Plurals

Provide each child with two paper plates and some die-cut cows. Have each child glue one cow on one of the plates and several cows on the other plate. Children can take turns holding up one of their plates to a partner and asking: *Am I holding up cowssss or cow?* **Note:** These plates can also be used as a Circle Time activity with the teacher asking children: Hold up cowssss. Hold up cow.

Materials: Shallow tub, brown paint, rubber worms, small nets

⚙ *Fine Motor*
Digging for Worms—Plurals

Fill a shallow tub with water, and add a squirt of brown paint so the water looks muddy. Purchase a number of rubber fishing worms and small nets. Invite children to reach in with their nets and get some worms. As they pull in their catch, ask children, Did you get *wormsss* or *worm?*

Materials: Tub-like container, large beads, small plastic containers or baby food jars with lids

⚙ *Sensory/Motor*
Beads and Jewels: Opposites—Full/Empty; Actions—Tense

Provide a tub filled with large beads and small plastic containers or baby-food jars with lids. Allow children time to explore. Then encourage children to fill the various containers with beads. Ask if the containers are *full* or *empty*. (Children can also take turns asking each other.) Show children a full container, and following the language for Actions/Tense, ask: Is this jar full? *Yes.* Now watch. (Empty the jar.) Is this jar full? *No.* Was this jar full? *Yes.*

Fine Motor
Puzzles—Part/Whole
Make puzzles of the objects learned in the Part/Whole exercises—toothbrush, table, pencil, wagon, elephant, tree, umbrella. Draw or make a photocopy of each object that includes all its parts. Glue the pictures on card stock. Cut the pictures apart to make puzzle pieces. Store each in a labeled resealable plastic bag. Encourage children to "say the whole thing" as they complete each puzzle.

Painting
Fall Leaf Prints—Matching
In advance, prepare four-inch poster-board squares—two per child. Provide a variety of freshly fallen leaves and various fall colors of paint. Have each child create a leaf print by painting the underside of a leaf and pressing it to the front of one of the squares. Then, have each child make an identical print on the remaining square. When the prints are dry, store them in a basket. Children can work individually or in small groups to find matching leaves in this class-made game.

Science
The Grass Is Greener
Collect a supply of half-pint milk cartons. Clean the cartons, and cut off the tops. Give each child a strip of paper that has been cut to match the height of the carton and is long enough to wrap around it. Have each child paint a strip green. While the paint is wet, sprinkle the strip with green glitter. When it's dry, children tape or glue the strip around a carton. Then, have children fill their cartons with soil. Finally, have each child press a spoonful of grass seed into the dirt. Place cartons in a sunny window, and watch the green grass grow.

Sorting
Vehicle Sort—Classification
Prepare picture cards using pictures of various vehicles, or use the Picture Cards. Mix these cards with Object cards, and encourage children to sort cards into two piles—*vehicle* or *not a vehicle*. Encourage children to use the word *vehicle* as you ask them about their sorted piles. **Note**: Add vehicles to your Block Center. Children enjoy building construction sites and garages.

Materials: Pictures of objects, card stock, glue, scissors, resealable plastic bags

Materials: Poster board, leaves, paints

Materials: Half-pint milk cartons, paper strips, green paint, green glitter, tape, glue, soil, grass seed

Materials: Picture Cards showing vehicles and objects

Materials:
Drawing paper,
crayons or
markers

 Writing

Hungry Caterpillars—Days of the Week

Children work in this center in groups of seven. Prepare several sets of drawing paper for each day of the week. Each group gets one set—Sunday through Saturday. At the top of each page, write *On (day of week), (name of child) ate* _____. Each child chooses one piece of paper with a day of the week on it. Children decide what they would eat if they were a hungry caterpillar. Then children draw a picture on their papers to illustrate their choice. As children tell you what they drew, write the word in the sentence blank. Staple these pages together, and encourage each group to share their completed "Days-of-the-Week" book with the class. Invite each child to "read" his or her page.

BOOKS FOR SHARED READING

The Very Hungry Caterpillar by Eric Carle

The Rainbow Fish by Marcus Pfister

Brown Cow, Green Grass, Yellow Mellow Sun by Ellen Jackson

Elmer by David McKee

Marmalade's Yellow Leaf by Cindy Wheeler

The Marvelous Mud Washing Machine by Patty Wolcott

Bears in Pairs by Niki Yektai

Airplanes by Byron Barton

Trucks by Byron Barton

Trains by Byron Barton

CIRCLE TIME

Hello, Children—Information—Days of the Week
(Teach this call-and-response song to the tune of "Frère Jacques.")
Hello, children. *Hello, teacher.*
Today is (day of week). *Today is (day of week).*
Tomorrow will be (day of week). *Tomorrow will be (day of week).*
Here at (name of school). *Here at (name of school).*

Vehicles, Vehicles—Classification
(Give each child a small, scale-model vehicle. Ask children:) What's the rule about vehicles? *If it is made to take you places, it is a vehicle.*
Listen. I'm going to name some vehicles, but don't let me fool you.
If I name something that is a vehicle, hold up your vehicle.
If I name something that is not a vehicle, say *not a vehicle.*

Flannel Board Fun—Part/Whole
(In advance, make flannel-board pieces for simple objects from the Part/Whole exercises. Call on a volunteer to place the parts for an object on the flannel board. Encourage the rest of the group to name the parts as the volunteer places them on the board. Example: As a student places the parts of a toothbrush, others respond:) *A toothbrush has bristles. A toothbrush has a handle.*

Pass the Hat—Classification—Vehicles/Food
(Put a variety of vehicle and food pictures from magazines [or use the Picture Cards] into a hat. Play music, and as the music plays, children pass the hat from one to another. Stop the music. The child holding the hat reaches in, pulls out a picture, and asks, *Vehicle* or *food?* The class responds.)

TRANSITIONS

On the Move!

Guess Who?
(Describe someone in the room by the clothes he or she is wearing. As soon as the child recognizes himself or herself, he or she jumps up and says:) *I'm the one!* (Child moves to the predetermined location.)

Let's Focus!

Parts of the Body—Language
(Say a word to children, and then have them repeat the word as they use different parts of their body to match the number of syllables:)
Vehicles, say it. *Vehicles.*
Say it with your hands. (Clap hands to syllables.)
Say it with your eyes. (Blink eyes to syllables.)
Say it with your feet. (Stamp feet to syllables.)
Say it with your head. (Move head back and forth to syllables.)

Observation—Review—Language
(Show a copy of a famous painting by Monet or Picasso, for example. Ask children to notice things about the picture, using concepts that have been taught. Ask:) What colors do you see? Are there short lines or long lines or both? Are there circles in the picture?

Listening
(To add some movement, sing the familiar song "If You're Happy and You Know It," adding new words such as these: If you're happy and you know it *point to a girl, throw a kiss, touch your nose,* and so on.)

CENTER ACTIVITIES

 Art

Flower Power—Part/Whole—Flower

Use the art materials listed to have the children make a model of a flower. Remind children that their model must include petals, roots, leaves, and stem.

Games

Vehicle Lotto—Object Identification/Classification

Follow the directions on page 36 of Language Activity Masters Book 1. Children make a simple lotto game to reinforce vehicle identification.

Listening/Speaking

Story Retell—Oral Language

Provide simple flannel-board pieces for a boy, a man, a shovel, shovels, hammers, and nails to go with "Dozy Brings the Shovels" from Storybook 2. As you reread the story, have children take turns adding flannel-board pieces on the board. Encourage children to take turns using the pieces and retelling the story in their own words. Invite other children to listen to the storyteller, and help them if any parts of the story are forgotten.

Listening/Speaking

Responding to Story

Have children listen to the recording of "Melissa Hides the Popcorn." A bowl of popcorn to eat while listening makes this activity more fun! Provide drawing paper and crayons, and ask children to draw their favorite part of the story. As children tell you about their pictures, write the words on their papers.

Math

Mellow Yellow Graph—Classification

Brainstorm with children to name foods they eat that are yellow. Provide a variety of these foods for children to taste—bananas, scrambled eggs, macaroni and cheese, corn bread, corn. Construct a simple picture graph on freezer paper of these foods. Give each child a die-cut yellow happy face, and have them personalize it. Then have each child indicate their favorite yellow food by placing a happy face in the appropriate space on the graph.

Materials: Construction paper, buttons, sunflower seeds, clay, yarn, chenille stems, scissors, glue

Materials: See Language Activity Masters Book 1 for BLM 70A and 70B and list of materials

Materials: Flannel board, flannel pieces from "Dozy Brings the Shovels"

Materials: Recording of "Melissa Hides the Popcorn" with children answering questions, popcorn for snacking, drawing paper, crayons

Materials: Yellow foods to taste (see activity), freezer paper, die-cut yellow happy faces

Materials:
Geoboards and
rubber bands

Math
Geoboard Triangles—Shape
Using the geoboards and rubber bands, encourage children to experiment with different ways to place the bands on the boards to form triangles.

Materials: Tub
of water, corks,
table tennis balls,
sponges, metal
spoons, rocks

Science
Sinkers and Floaters—Opposites
Develop activities using sinking and floating objects. Provide a tub of water and assorted items such as corks (or items made of cork), table tennis balls, sponges, metal spoons or other utensils, rocks, and so on. Encourage children to predict which items will sink and which will float. Then invite the children to test their predictions and to sort the items into two groups—sinkers and floaters. For another activity, provide children with clay and a tub of water. Have children make a clay object that will sink and a clay object that will float. Encourage children to share their explanations as to why one object will sink and another object will float.

Materials: A
plastic circle, a
paper circle, a
cloth circle; a box;
objects made of
plastic, paper,
and cloth

Sorting
Feel for a Match—Materials
Put three circles on a table—one made of plastic, one of paper, and one of cloth. Provide a box with a hole cut in it so children can reach in. Inside the box, place a variety of objects—some made of plastic, some of paper, and some of cloth. Children reach into the box, pull out an object, and place it on the circle made of the matching material.

Materials:
Overhead
projector; red,
yellow, and
green overhead
projector markers;
overheads
showing pictures
of objects *first*,
next, and *last*
in a line

Writing
Spatial First, Next, Last
Place an overhead projector on a low table or on the floor. Provide red, yellow, and green overhead projector markers. Prepare several simple overheads showing pictures of objects *first*, *next*, and *last* in a line. Encourage children to play in pairs with one child telling his or her partner to: *Make a yellow mark on (name of object) that is first in line. Make a red mark on (name of object) that is next in line. Make a green mark on (name of object) that is last in line.* Have partners switch roles and play again.

Materials:
Drawing paper,
crayons, stapler

Writing
Brown Bear Class Book—Identification and Colors
In groups of seven, make a class book following the familiar *Brown Bear, Brown Bear, What Do You See?* format. Brainstorm with children to name seven animals not used in the original story. Then let children assign a color to each of these

animals. Use colors taught—yellow, red, blue, black, orange, green, brown. Invite each child to draw one of the animals and then color it. (Example: blue fox.) Staple pages together, and encourage each group to share its book by "reading" it to the class. *Blue fox, blue fox, what do you see? I see an orange monkey looking at me.*

BOOKS FOR SHARED READING

Backyard Sunflower by Elizabeth King
From Seed to Plant by Gail Gibbons
Ten Seeds by Ruth Brown
Planting a Rainbow by Lois Ehlert
Float and Sink by Maria Gordon
Boats Afloat by Shelly Rotner
Busy Monday Morning by Janina Domanska
Growing Vegetable Soup by Lois Ehlert
Lunch by Denise Fleming
Colors by Heidi Goennel

CIRCLE TIME

Two Little Blackbirds—Opposites

(Teach the rhyme "Two Little Blackbirds," substituting the following words and adding actions:)

Two Little Blackbirds play the opposites game. (Place two fingers on top of hand.)

Empty and Full are the little birds' names. Fly away, Empty. (One finger moves off hand.) Fly away, Full. (The other finger moves off hand.)

Come back, Empty. (One finger returns to hand.) Come back, Full. (Other finger returns to hand.)

(Repeat rhyme using other opposites taught: short/long, wet/dry, big/small, young/old.)

Name That Material!—Materials

(Fill a hat or bag with small objects made of a variety of materials taught— plastic, glass, wood, cloth. Play music as children pass the bag around the circle. When the music stops, the child holding the bag reaches in, pulls out an object, and names the material the object is made of.)

Hokey Pokey—Shapes

(Give each child a small circle and a small triangle cutout. Children stand and form a circle, placing the shapes by their feet. Sing "The Hokey-Pokey," substituting these words:)

You put your circle in. (Children pick up circle shape and hold it in the circle.)

You put your circle out. (Children move circle shape out of the circle.)

You put your circle in, and you shake it all about. (Children put circle shape in circle and shake it.)

You do the Hokey-Pokey, and you turn yourself around. (Children hold circle and turn around.)

That's what it's all about! (Children place circle back at their feet. Repeat the song using triangle shape.)

Pay Attention—Review: What's Missing

(Choose several articles of clothing—shoes, hats, shirt, belt. Name each object as you place it in a basket. Cover the basket with a towel, and describe one of the objects. Ask children to name the object you described. Ask one child to come to the basket and take out that article of clothing.)

TRANSITIONS

On the Move!

What Goes With That?—Classification
(Hold up a spoon. Ask children what goes with a spoon. Answers may include a dish, a fork, food, and so on. Hold up another object. As children make an association, they move to the next activity or line up.)

Hello/Good-bye—Vocabulary
(Before children move from one activity to another, talk about different ways to say good-bye or hello. Ideas: Wave, say, "Bye," "See you later," and so on. Give each child a turn to say "good-bye" or "hello," and then move to the next activity.)

Let's Focus!

Building Vocabulary—Yes/No
(Pick an occupation that children have learned —dentist, firefighter, teacher. Review the rule for each occupation. Then ask questions requiring a *yes* or *no* answer:)
Have you ever gone to a dentist? *Yes.* Does a dentist make ice cream? *No.*

Can You Hear Me?—Actions
(To regain children's attention, softly say:) If you can hear me, touch your head. (Use any quiet action. As children hear you, they stop, get quiet, and do the action. Watch how quickly the quiet settles around your room!)

CENTER ACTIVITIES

Art

Crisscross Mobile—Common Information (Use after lesson 75.)

Follow the directions on page 39 of Language Activity Masters Book 1 to make mobiles that tell about the sky, land, sun, and clouds.

Dramatic Play

Acting Out a Story

Give a small group of children one or more props to use with the book *If You Take a Mouse to School.* Read the story aloud, and have children hold up their props at the proper time. After repeated readings, encourage children to work together in small groups and retell the story on their own to the rest of the class.

Common Information—Grocery Store

Set up a Grocery Store Center next to your Housekeeping Center. Provide a table for the checkout counter and empty shelving to stack different foods. Additional ideas for props are aprons for the storekeepers, cash register, play money, calculators, shopping cart, empty food containers, foam trays for pretend food, paper for shopping list, grocery ads, coupons, adding-machine paper rolls, sacks or bags, pencils and pens.

Games

Shape Game—Circles and Triangles

Prepare twenty index cards. On ten cards draw circles; on ten cards draw triangles. Make a simple path-like game board on poster board. Divide the game board into squares. Have a "Start" and a "Finish" point, and indicate the direction of movement with an arrow if necessary. In each square draw a circle or a triangle. Children play this game in pairs. Each child needs a game marker (coin, bean, button) that he or she places on "Start." Place the shuffled index cards in the middle of the game board. Taking turns, a child draws a card, names the shape, and moves his or her marker to the next matching shape on the game board. Play continues until each child reaches the finish.

🧹 *Housekeeping*

Cooking—Top/Middle/Bottom

In advance, fill small clear cups about one-third full of blue or green gelatin. Provide gummy fish and whipped cream to follow a three-step recipe. Prepare three simple picture cards: one showing a cup with gelatin, one showing gummy fish on top of the gelatin, one showing whipped cream on top of the gummy fish. On a table, put an arrow made from colored tape. Place the recipe picture cards above the arrow. Review the recipe with children. What do you do first? What do you do next? What do you do last? Invite children to follow the recipe and make the treat. After children finish making their treats, ask them to identify what is on *top*, in the *middle*, and at the *bottom*.

⚙️ *Fine Motor*

Pair Relations

Make an even number of cards from card stock. Glue pictures of animals on half of the cards and pictures of animal homes on the other half. Provide spring-type clothespins. Encourage children to match animals and their homes using clothespins to clip the pairs together. Vary this activity by making cards for other categories of pairs such as pictures of opposites (long/short), pictures of nouns that go together (bat/ball), and matching action pictures (swimming).

⚙️ ## Plurals

Supply a number of die-cut triangles and circles. Using a hole punch, punch one hole in some of the triangles and circles. Punch several holes in the remaining triangles and circles. Encourage children to sort the shapes according to *hole* or *holes*. After the shapes are sorted, give each child a piece of yarn. Invite children to string the shapes with one hole onto the yarn to make "shape" necklaces.

🌐 *Social Studies*

Facts about Our State

Read simple books containing information about your state. Discuss unique features of the state and things you can find and do in your state. For example, Florida is the Sunshine State; Ohio is the Buckeye State. Draw a large outline of your state on freezer paper. On separate pieces of paper, encourage children to draw something they learned about their state. Glue these pictures on the freezer paper, and display the completed map. Put a large star on the map where your city, town, or area is located.

Materials: Index cards, clear plastic cups, blue or green gelatin, gummy fish, whipped cream, colored tape

Materials: Card stock, pictures of animals and animal homes, spring-type clothespins

Materials: Die-cut triangles and circles, hole punch, yarn

Materials: Facts about your state, freezer paper, drawing paper, glue

Materials:
Freezer paper,
old magazines,
or laminated
pictures from the
Classification
track

○○
● *Sorting*
Classification
Divide a piece of freezer paper into four sections. Label and illustrate each section with a Classification concept—container, vehicle, food, clothing. Have children cut pictures from magazines to represent each of the categories. Working in small groups, children place their pictures on the freezer paper under the appropriate heading. To make this center reusable, photocopy and laminate pictures from the Classification exercises in *Language for Learning*. Add additional Classification concepts as they are taught.

Materials: Light
green and dark
green
construction
paper, crayons

✎ *Writing*
Green Thumbs—Oral Language: Classification
Ask children to brainstorm to name a list of things that can be green. Write each child's idea on a large, light green leaf made from construction paper. Then ask children to illustrate their "green" ideas on their leaves. Glue the illustrated light green leaves onto slightly larger leaves cut from dark green paper.

BOOKS FOR SHARED READING

Tommy at the Grocery Store by Bill Grossman

Do the Doors Open by Magic? And Other Supermarket Questions
    by Catherine Ripley

Curious George Goes to School by Margret and H. A. Rey

Teachers Help Us Learn by Carol Greene

Froggy Goes to School by Jonathan London

I Want to Be a Firefighter by Edith Kunhardt

Fire Fighters by Norma Simon

Find Your Coat, Ned by Pam Zinnemann-Hope

Let's Go Shopping, Ned by Pam Zinnemann-Hope

Spots, Feathers, and Curly Tails by Nancy Tafuri

CIRCLE TIME

I Spy—Shapes: Circle, Triangle, Rectangle, Square
(Play I spy using shapes. Have one child in the group begin by giving a clue for an object in the classroom that includes a shape. For example, child says:) *I spy something that is a circle.*

I Will Buy . . . Predictable Chart—Common Information
(Review with children the definition *A store is a place where you buy things.* To reinforce classification skills, ask children to think of things they could buy at a grocery store. On chart paper, write **I will buy** _____. Then complete the sentence with a grocery store item. Give each child a turn to dictate a sentence as you write it on the chart. Put the child's name at the end of the sentence. **Note:** This chart can be used later in the Writing Center with the activity Class Book.)

Roll On—Classification
(Prepare a cube with pictures representing the Classification concepts learned so far—foods, vehicles, containers, clothing, animals. Children take turns rolling the cube to each other. The child who receives the cube identifies the class of the picture that lands faceup. Then the group says the rule for that class.)

Silly Moves—Actions: And
(Combine movements children can have fun with:) Everybody, hop and clap. What are you doing? *Hopping and clapping.* Say the whole thing. (Other examples of fun action combinations might be:) Stand up, and hold your leg straight out in front of you. Point to something blue, and point to something yellow.

TRANSITIONS

On the Move!

That's Me!
(Print each child's name on a colored sentence strip. Hold up the name strips one at a time. When children see their names they say:) *That's me!* (Child then moves to line up or to go to the next activity.)

Color Crowns
(See "Colorful Crowns" in Center Activities. Have children wear their crowns. Then using the colors of the crowns, call on children to line up or to go to a small group activity.)

Let's Focus!

(Teacher begins this activity by chanting a simple pattern and adding hand motions. First, chant:) Dum, dum, da, da. (Then add motions as you continue the chant:) Clap, clap, tap knees, tap knees. (Children repeat the chant and the motion pattern with you. Vary the chant by speeding it up or slowing it down. Change the pattern to just the motions without the chant.)

CENTER ACTIVITIES

Art
Colorful Crowns—Colors
Provide large pieces of construction paper in the various colors children have learned so far. Encourage children to choose a color and make a crown-type hat. Help each child staple his or her hat to fit. (Use the crowns for the On the Move! transition activity above.)

Rainbow Puppets—Common Information and Colors
Give each child a die-cut shape of a sun and a cloud. Have children attach a craft stick to each shape. Provide white paper cut in the shape of a rainbow. Encourage children to color their rainbows. Then help children fold their rainbows accordion style. Next instruct children to glue one end of the rainbow to the sun and the other end to the cloud so each rainbow is sandwiched between the sun and the cloud. Children can make their rainbows appear and disappear as they "open and close" the sun and the cloud.

Dramatic Play
Common Information
Stock your dramatic play area with props that could be used by a dentist, firefighter, and teacher. Include clothing items if possible. Encourage children to dress as one of these individuals and role-play the part. As you circulate, ask children what they know about a dentist, firefighter, and teacher. Example: What do we call a person who puts out fires? *A firefighter.* Say the whole thing about a firefighter. *A firefighter is a person who puts out fires.*

Games
Opposites
Construct a game board by photocopying pictures from the Opposites track. Make sure you have pairs of opposites (wet/dry, long/short). Separate the pairs into two sets. Glue one set of pictures to poster board, making a game board with "Start" and "Finish." Laminate and stack the other set of pictures. Each child needs a game marker. To play, a child draws a card from the stack and moves his or her marker to the closest picture that shows the *opposite* of the card drawn. Encourage children to say the opposite word as they move their markers.

Housekeeping
Fill up the Refrigerator!—Containers—Top-Middle-Bottom—Object Identification
Give each child a copy of BLM 85. Follow the directions on page 44 of Language Activity Masters Book 1 to make a refrigerator filled with foods. Children place pictures of food items cut from magazines and grocery store ads on the *top*, *middle*, and *bottom* shelves.

Materials:
Drawing paper,
crayons

📞 *Listening/Speaking*

Responding to a Story

Record the story "Melissa Will Try" in Storybook 2. After children listen to the story, encourage them to draw a picture of something that they have had to try very hard to learn to do. Invite them to share their pictures with the rest of the class.

Materials: Paper
bags, attribute
shapes

🧮 *Math*

Feel a Shape—Circle, Triangle, Rectangle, Square

Children play this game in pairs. For each pair, prepare a paper bag with the four different attribute shapes inside. One child reaches into the bag, feels a shape, and describes it to the partner. The partner names the shape. The child then pulls the shape out of the bag to see if the guess was correct. Partners switch roles, and play continues.

Materials: Mirror,
clear container,
water, overhead
projector

🧪 *Science*

Rainbows—Common Information and Color

Fill the clear container three-fourths full of water, and place it on the overhead. Hold the mirror in the water, and angle it slightly back and forth until a spectrum of light is produced on the ceiling. Explain to children that a rainbow can be seen in the sky when the sun shines through raindrops in just the right way. Talk about the colors of the spectrum.

Materials:
Collection of
small objects
made of various
materials

⚫ *Sorting*

What's that Material?

Use the collection of small objects representing the materials learned so far—cloth, wood, plastic, metal, leather. Encourage children to sort the objects into groups according to the material from which they are made. As you circulate, ask children about their sorts.

Materials:
Drawing paper,
crayons

✏️ *Writing*

Class Book—Common Information

Using the I Will Buy . . . Predictable Chart from the Circle Time activity, write each child's sentence at the bottom of a piece of drawing paper. Include child's name, or have children write their own names if they are able. Read each child's sentence aloud to remind the child what he or she planned to buy. Encourage children to draw a picture of their item. Make a cover titled "At the Grocery Store," and staple all pages together, including an additional blank page, to create a class book. Type simple directions to family members asking them to write a sentence on the last page of the book telling what *they* would buy at the grocery store. Allow a different child to take the book home each night. As children bring the book back to school each morning, they share with the class what their family members would buy.

BOOKS FOR SHARED READING

I Know a Dentist by Naomi Barnett

My Dentist by Harlow Rockwell

It Looked Like Spilt Milk by Charles G. Shaw

Little Cloud by Eric Carle

My First Wild Animals by Bettina Paterson

This Is the Farmer by Nancy Tafuri

Sun, Rain by Niki Yektai

Quick as a Cricket by Audrey Wood

Wet World by Norma Simon

The Cloud Book by Tomie dePaola

CIRCLE TIME

What's Missing?—Materials
(Show children a tray with five objects on it that are all made of the same material. Use materials taught so far—cloth, paper, plastic, glass, wood, metal, leather, concrete. Ask children to identify the material from which the objects are made. Then have them name each object. Ask children to cover their eyes as you remove one object. Have children open their eyes, and ask:) What's missing? (Repeat the game using the same objects, but remove two items at a time. Change the items on the tray, and continue the game using objects made of a different material.)

Beach Ball—Classification
(In advance, cut pictures from magazines that show the Classification concepts taught so far—container, vehicle, food, clothing, animals. Glue a different picture on each of the colored sections of an inflated beach ball. Children sit in a circle and roll the ball back and forth to each other. As each child receives the ball, he or she identifies the object in the picture under his or her hand and the class it is in.)

Animals, Animals—Object Identification and Colors
(Give each child in the circle a different colored stuffed animal. Hold a brown bear, and start the chant:) Brown bear, brown bear, what do you see? I see a/an [name the color and the animal a child is holding]. (Example: Orange giraffe. The child holding the named animal continues the chant with:) *Orange giraffe, orange giraffe, what do you see? I see a/an (name the color and animal that another child is holding).* (Continue until all children have had a turn.)

TRANSITIONS

On the Move!

Common Information
(Show children a globe or a map of Earth. Explain which parts are *land* and which parts are *oceans*. Give each child a turn to identify *land* or *ocean* as you touch different spots on the globe. As each child identifies *land* or *ocean,* he or she lines up or moves to the next activity.)

Part/Whole
(Photocopy pictures of objects from the Part/Whole exercises—house, shoe, wagon, elephant. Cut the objects into parts, and give each child a part. Say:) Let's name the parts of a house. (Children holding the parts of a house stand up and bring their parts to you one at a time, as they say:) *A house has a (door, window, roof, walls).* (Continue until all children are in line or at the next activity.)

Let's Focus!

Some/All/None
(To gain children's attention, say:) Listen. Am I holding up *some* of my fingers, *all* of my fingers, or *none* of my fingers? (Once children are looking at you, continue to hold up *some, all,* or *none* or your fingers. Children answer *some, all,* or *none.* Repeat several times, varying the number of fingers you are holding up.)

CENTER ACTIVITIES

Materials: Round balloons, papier-mâché materials, globe of Earth, brown and green paint

✂ *Art*
Common Information—Earth/Ocean

In small groups of three or four, have children cover a round balloon with strips of papier-mâché. Allow these to dry, and then pop the balloon. Provide a globe of Earth for children to look at as they paint their globes using brown or green to show land masses and blue to show oceans. As children work, circulate and ask them to tell you the information they have learned about *Earth, land,* and *oceans.*

Materials: Variety of shoes and boots, shoe brushes, shoe boxes, shoe horns, socks, a foot measuring device (a ruler), sponges for polishing, shoelaces, cash register, play money

🐾 *Dramatic Play*
Shoe Store

For a change of pace, turn your grocery store into a shoe store. Provide props that would be found in a shoe store. As children play, ask questions such as: What size shoes do you wear? What kind of shoes do you need? What are the parts of a shoe?

Materials: Index cards or card stock, magnetic tape, magnetic boards or cookie sheets

♟ *Games*
Opposites

Make picture cards showing opposites learned so far—full and empty, big and small, wet and dry, short and long, old and young. Place a piece of magnetic tape on the back of each picture. Using magnetic boards or cookie sheets, direct children to arrange the opposite pairs beside each other. Then ask children to name the opposites.

Materials: Round crackers, green-tinted frosting, pretzel sticks, small red candies, rebus recipe for making an apple tree

🧹 *Housekeeping*
Cooking—Make an Orchard

To reinforce the new Common Information about an orchard—an orchard is a place where fruit trees are grown—have children make edible apple trees. Provide a round cracker, green-tinted frosting, a pretzel stick, and small red candies for each child. Children follow the steps on the rebus recipe. The first pictured instruction shows icing the cracker with green frosting. The next picture shows adding the pretzel trunk. The last instruction shows adding the small red candy apples. As children follow the recipe, have them "say the whole thing" about an orchard.

☏ Listening
Responding to a Story (Use after lesson 97.)
After children listen to the recording of the story "Denise Builds a House," encourage them to draw a picture of the house that Denise built. Remind them to include windows, doors, walls, and roof.

Materials: Recording of "Denise Builds a House" from Storybook 3, drawing paper

🖩 Math
Materials—Sort and Graph
Provide a simple picture graph with headings showing materials—cloth, paper, glass, plastic, metal, wood, concrete. Have children work in pairs. Using old magazines, encourage children to cut out pictures of things made of the materials listed on the graph and place them under the appropriate headings. Children can also draw their own pictures on the graph. Encourage each pair of children to tell the rest of the class about their graph.

Materials: Poster board for graph showing materials

⚙ Fine Motor
Sorting: Opposites—Big/Small
Provide several plates filled with a variety of different sizes of seeds. For each child, prepare a large index card or piece of card stock with the top half labeled "Big" and the bottom half labeled "Small." Encourage children to sort the seeds into two piles—big and small. Each child then glues the big seeds at the top and the small seeds at the bottom of their card. Encourage children to tell about what their cards show.

Materials: Plates, different sizes of seeds, large index cards or card stock, glue

✎ Painting
Common Information—Firefighters
Provide drawing paper and dot markers in orange, red, and yellow. Invite children to use these markers to "paint" a fire on their paper. When their paintings are dry, encourage children to draw a firefighter using a hose to spray water on the fire. Have children "say the whole thing" about a firefighter: *A firefighter is a person who puts out fires.*

Materials: Drawing paper; red, orange, and yellow dot markers; crayons

⚗ Science
Make a Cloud
Demonstrate this experiment to small groups of children. Fill the large glass jar with hot water. Pour out all the water except for about one inch. As soon as you pour off the water, wrap the thin cloth over the mouth of the jar. Put some ice on top of the cloth. A cloud will form in the jar above the water. As a follow-up activity, take children outside. Give each child a clipboard and drawing paper. Ask children to look at the clouds and draw them. Repeat this over several days to get examples of the different types of clouds.

Materials: Large glass jar, hot water, a thin cloth, ice, clipboards, drawing paper, crayons

Materials:
Drawing paper, stapler

Writing

Common Information—Occupation

Show children pictures from the Common Information track of occupations they have learned—dentist, firefighter, teacher, carpenter. Ask children to draw a picture showing the type of work they would like to do. After children draw their pictures, ask them to tell why they would like to do the job they chose. Record their sentences above their pictures. Make a cover titled "Occupations," and staple these pages together, including an additional blank page, to create a class book. Give each child an opportunity to take the book home and ask a parent or another adult to write a sentence describing their job. As children bring the book back to school each morning, invite them to share with the class the jobs their parents or family members wrote about.

BOOKS FOR SHARED READING

Even Firefighters Hug Their Moms by Christine Kole MacLean

Big Sarah's Little Boots by Paulette Bourgeois

Shoes from Grandpa by Mem Fox

Shoe Town by Janet Stevens and Susan Stevens Crummel

The Seasons of Arnold's Apple Tree by Gail Gibbons

Brian Wildsmith's Farm Animals by Brian Wildsmith

Farm Lift the Flap by Hinkler Books

People Working by Douglas Florian

City Street by Douglas Florian

Rosie's Walk by Pat Hutchins

CIRCLE TIME

In a People House—Predictable Chart—Part/Whole

(Review the parts of a house—walls, roof, windows, door. Then discuss with children the things we see in a house. On chart paper, write the sentence **You see** _____. Then complete the sentence with something you see in a house. Give each child a turn to dictate a sentence as you write it on the chart. Put the child's name at the end of the sentence. Example: *You see chairs, Tom.* **Note:** This chart can be used later in the Writing Center with the activity class book.)

Pass the Hat—Locations

(Children sit in a circle. Use the Picture Cards or pictures from magazines for locations taught—city, farm, store, forest, orchard. Place these pictures in a hat. As music plays, children pass the hat. When the music stops, the child holding the hat reaches in, pulls out a location card, holds it up, and names the location. Example: *City.* Then everyone says the definition. *A city is a place with lots of people.*)

Some, All, None

(Ask four or five volunteers to stand up. Ask questions using the language from the Some/All/None format. For example:) Are **all** of these children wearing red? Are **some** of these children wearing red? Are **none** of these children wearing red? (Children respond with *yes* or *no*.)

TRANSITIONS

On the Move!

Opposites
(Use Picture Card pairs showing opposites taught—full/empty, big/small, wet/dry, long/short, old/young, tall/short. [Use the cards you made for "Games—Opposites" in the Center Activities for lessons 91–100.] Give each child one card. Some children will have the same picture. When you hold up a Picture Card showing *full*, children with a Picture Card showing *empty* hold up their cards, bring them to you, and line up or go to the next activity.)

Let's Focus!

Actions/Prepositions
(To gain children's attention, play Simon says using prepositions taught—on, under, over, in front of, in back of, next to, between. Examples:) Simon says, Hold your hand *over* your head. Put all your fingers *on* your face.

Critical Thinking/Oral Language
(Ask children questions, and tell them to respond either "yes" by shaking head up and down or "no" by shaking head back and forth. Examples:) Is a strawberry brown? Do monkeys wear dresses? Does candy taste good?

CENTER ACTIVITIES

✂ *Art*
Occupation—Carpenter
Each child will need a copy of BLM 100A and 100B from Language Activity Masters Book 1, one sheet of 8½ × 11-inch cardboard, crayons, scissors, glue, and five pieces of hook-and-loop tape cut into half-inch pieces. Follow the directions on page 51 of Language Activity Masters Book 1. Children will make a carpenter and carpenter's tools. As children are working, ask: What do we call a person who builds things out of wood? *A carpenter.*

📌 *Games*
Sequencing—First/Before/After
Provide a set of commercially made sequence cards, or make your own three-step sequencing cards. For example, show: 1) Digging a hole; 2) Putting seeds in the hole; 3) A plant sprouting. Children can work individually or in pairs to put sets of cards in the correct sequence. As they work, ask children questions such as: What happened *first*? *A hole was dug.* What happened *before* the plant sprouted? *Seeds were put in the ground.* What happened *after* the seeds were put in the ground? *A plant sprouted.*

🧹 *Housekeeping*
Cooking—Bear Faces—First/Next and Before/After
Give each child a slice of bread, peanut butter, three slices of banana, raisins, and a plastic table knife. Provide a rebus recipe showing the following three steps in making a bear face: 1) Spreading peanut butter on bread; 2) Placing a banana slice on the top left and top right of bread for ears, and one slice in the middle for the snout; and 3) Adding eyes, nose (nostrils), and mouth using the raisins. After children have made their bear snacks, ask: What did you do *first? Spread the peanut butter.* What did you do *next? Made ears and a snout with banana slices.* What did you do *after* you made the ears and the snout? *Made eyes, nose, and mouth.* As children look at the rebus recipe steps, ask questions such as: What did you do *before* you made the ears and snout? What did you do *after* you spread the peanut butter?

📞 *Listening/Speaking*
Story Retelling—My Balloon
Use the poem "My Balloon" from Storybook 3, and say it as an echo poem. Say the words in a normal voice, and have children repeat the words in a softer voice: My big, red balloon. *My big, red balloon.* Was up in a tree. *Was up in a tree.* Who got my balloon? *Who got my balloon?* It wasn't me. *It wasn't me.* Provide flannel board cutouts of a tree, a red balloon, and a monkey. Encourage children to take turns putting the cutouts on the flannel board as they recite the poem.

Materials: (see activity)

Materials: Sequence cards

Materials: Index cards, bread, peanut butter, bananas, raisins, plastic table knives

Materials: Flannel board, flannel board cutouts of tree, red balloon, monkey

Materials:
Recording of "The Strongest Animal in the Jungle" including student responses, drawing paper

Listening/Speaking

Responding to a Story

Record the story "The Strongest Animal in the Jungle" from Storybook 3. Include children's responses to the questions asked throughout the reading. Place the recording in the Listening/Speaking Center. After children listen to the recording, provide drawing paper, and encourage each child to draw a picture of the strongest animal in the jungle. Give children an opportunity to tell why they chose to draw their animals.

Materials:
Freezer paper, commercially-made crackers in assorted shapes

Math

Graphing Shapes

Provide each child with a small bag of crackers in assorted shapes—circles, rectangles, triangles, squares. Have each child sort the crackers by shape. Using a piece of freezer paper, prepare a class graph with the cracker shapes as headings. After sorting crackers, have children place their crackers on the class graph under the appropriate headings.

Materials: Three-inch diameter paper circles, pictures of objects from the Classification track

Fine Motor

Pancake Flip—Classification

Prepare a set of circles that are three inches in diameter. Make pairs using pictures of objects children have learned from the Classification track—vehicles, food, containers, clothing, animals, buildings. Glue a picture to one side of each circle. Provide a plastic spatula. To play, turn all the cards facedown. Using the spatula, a child flips over two cards. If the two cards are in the same class, the child identifies the class and keeps the two cards. Play continues with children taking turns flipping "pancakes" until all matches are found.

Materials: Blue bulletin board paper, spray adhesive, table salt, finger paints, fish and whale shapes, wiggle eyes, glue

Painting

Ocean

From the Common Information track, review the location information: *an ocean is a place with lots of salt water*. Create an ocean mural. Cut a length of blue bulletin board paper. Put spray adhesive on the paper, and have children sprinkle salt over it. Next give children paper, and have them use finger paints to paint their papers various colors. Allow papers to dry. Provide cardboard shapes of fish or whales for children to trace around on the finger-painted papers, and then cut them out. Have children add a wiggle eye to each fish or whale, and then glue their finished products onto the blue bulletin board ocean background.

Science
Fruit and Seeds
From the Common Information track, reinforce *orchard* and *fruit.* Give each child a plate with half an apple, two grapes, and one cherry. Have children use their fingers to remove the seeds from each piece of fruit and place them on a paper towel to dry. Allow children to eat the fruit samples. Give each child a piece of paper with simple drawings of an apple, grapes, and a cherry. Direct children to color the drawings and glue each type of dried seed on the appropriate picture. As children work, ask, Which type of fruit has the biggest (or smallest) seeds? Why do you think some fruits have smaller seeds than others? Say the whole thing about an orchard. *An orchard is a place with lots of fruit trees.*

Materials: Apples, grapes, cherries, paper plates, paper towels, crayons, glue

Writing
Class Book—Part/Whole
Using the In a People House—Predictable Chart from the Circle Time activity, write each child's sentence at the bottom of a piece of drawing paper. Include child's name, or have children write their own names if they are able. Read each sentence aloud to remind the children of what they said they would see in a house. Encourage children to draw a picture of their object. Make a cover titled "In a People House," and staple all pages together, including an additional blank page, to create a class book. Type simple directions to family members asking them to write a sentence on the last page of the book that names something *they* see in their own house. Allow a different child to take the book home each night. The next morning in Circle Time, the child shares the family member's sentence or comment.

Materials: Drawing paper

BOOKS FOR SHARED READING
Exactly the Opposite by Tana Hoban

Is It Rough? Is It Smooth? Is It Shiny? by Tana Hoban

In a People House by Dr. Seuss

The Wonderful House by Margaret Wise Brown

The Shape of Things by Dale Ann Dodds

When a Line Bends . . . A Shape Begins by Rhonda Gowler Greene

Over in the Ocean by Jack Hartmann

The Ocean Alphabet Book by Jerry Pallotta

Doctor Tools by Inez Snyder

Corduroy Goes to the Doctor by Don Freeman

CIRCLE TIME

Jump-Up—Shapes
(On blank cards, draw shapes children have learned, or use the shape cards from the Picture Cards box. Also prepare three cards that show a jumping stick figure. To play Jump-Up, show children one card at a time. If the card shows a shape, children name the shape. If the card shows the jumping stick figure, children jump to their feet and then sit back down. Common objects, colors, and objects from the Classification exercises can be reviewed the same way.)

Lily Pad—Actions—Prepositions
(Give each child a lily pad cut from green paper or craft foam. Ask them to hold their lily pads *over, in front of, in back of, under, next to, between* or *on* different body parts—abdomen, arm, leg, hip, foot, chest, elbow, neck, head, hand. Make the game more challenging by asking children to do two-step directions such as:) Put one hand on your lily pad and one hand on the floor. (For another variation, incorporate the word *or* in the directions. For example:) Put your knee on your lily pad *or* on the floor. (**Note:** Shapes can be used in place of lily pads.)

Wagon Load—Part/Whole—Materials
(Bring a child-size wagon to circle time. Load it with real objects from the Part/Whole and Materials exercises—umbrella, belt, broom, toy car, saw, toothbrush, shoe, hammer, nail. First ask children to identify the parts of the wagon and the materials the parts are made of. Then let each child take a turn holding up one of the items in the wagon, and call on other children to name the parts and the materials they are made of. Continue until all children have had a turn.)

TRANSITIONS

On the Move!

Classification
(Play a Classification game. Name a class—food, plants, vehicles, buildings, animals, containers. Call on individual children to name an object in the specified class. As children name an object, they line up or go to the next activity.)

Let's Focus!

Materials
(Play the Wagon Load materials game from Circle Time to focus attention or while waiting in line. Name a material—glass, wood, rubber, leather. Call on individual children to name something made out of that material.)

CENTER ACTIVITIES

✂ Art

Parts of a House

Encourage children to use pretzel sticks to make a house by arranging the sticks and gluing them on the paper. Remind children to include roof, walls, windows, and door.

Games

Slapjack—Opposites

Make a set of picture cards to go with the opposites taught—full/empty, big/small, wet/dry, long/short, old/young, tall/short. To play, two children sit facing each other. One opposite card from each pair of opposites is faceup between them. A caller has the other set of cards containing the corresponding opposites. The caller names an opposite—for example, *Full*. Each player tries to be the first to slap the appropriate opposite card—*Empty*. The first child to slap the correct card keeps it. Play continues until all cards have been slapped.

☎ Listening/Speaking

Responding to a Story

Record a reading of *Rumble in the Jungle*. After listening to the story, encourage children to name different animals that were in the story. Invite children to draw their favorite jungle animal. Ask children why they liked that particular animal, and write their responses on their pictures.

🧮 Math

Measuring—Graphing

Plant a fast-growing bulb such as an amaryllis in a small pot, and place it near a window. When the stem has sprouted from the bulb, begin to measure the plant's growth each day. Children take turns measuring the height of the plant using a strip of construction paper and marking it where the strip touches the top of the plant. Cut it at that point. Glue the strip at the bottom edge and near the left margin of a large piece of paper to begin a growth chart. Each day add another strip to the chart. Soon children will see the growth of the plant as shown on their bar graph.

⚙ Motor

Bowling—Some/All/None

Make a bowling game to be played in the classroom or on the playground. Clean ten or more empty quart milk containers, and fill with sand. Provide a ball heavy enough to knock over the cartons. Arrange the containers in a triangle formation like the pins at a bowling alley. Children roll the ball and tell if they knocked over *some, all,* or *none* of the "bowling pins."

Fine Motor

Names—Matching

Label a photo of each child with his or her name, and glue the photo on the pocket of a pocket chart. Write each letter of the child's name on individual cards. Place the group of letters in the pocket behind the child's photo. Children study each photo and name, and arrange the groups of letters in the pocket behind the photo to spell the appropriate child's name.

Materials: Individual photos, cards with each letter of a child's name, pocket chart

 Painting

Jungle

Make a jungle mural using a large piece of green bulletin board paper. Have children sponge paint jungle trees and grass using shades of green and brown paint. Talk about animals found in the jungle. Using the animal shapes, children trace around, cut out, and paint their jungle animals and glue them on the mural to complete their classroom jungle scene.

Materials: Green bulletin board paper, sponges, green and brown paint, animal shapes to trace, scissors, glue

 *Science*

Plants

Provide each small group with hand lenses; a real plant that shows roots, stem, leaves, and flowers; and drawing paper for each child. Encourage children to use the hand lenses to observe and study the parts of a plant. Then have each child draw a picture of a plant and use it to identify the plant's parts.

Materials: Hand lenses, plants, drawing paper

 *Sorting*

Same/Different

Focus on similarities and differences by cutting a large supply of strips from various types of paper—construction paper, wrapping paper, wallpaper, tissue paper, newspaper. Include strips that are the same color or size but from different kinds of paper. Working in small groups, children discover how the strips are the *same* and how they are *different*. Have students sort their strips by one attribute—color, size, or paper type. Have them glue each set on a separate sheet of paper. Ask each group to show their paper to the class and explain how the strips are sorted.

Materials: Paper strips of various types and colors, sheets of construction paper, glue

Writing

Occupations

Read the book *Guess Who?* by Margaret Miller. Talk with children about the jobs in the book they think are the most interesting. Encourage children to draw a picture of a worker they learned about in the book. Have each child dictate a sentence to you that tells what the worker in their picture does. Write it on their picture. Encourage children to share their pictures and sentences with the rest of the class.

Materials: *Guess Who?* by Margaret Miller, drawing paper, crayons or markers

BOOKS FOR SHARED READING

Rumble in the Jungle by Giles Andreae

Jungle Boogie by Sally Crabtree

Guess Who? by Margaret Miller

We're Different, We're the Same by Bobbi Kates

Sneetches Are Sneetches: Learn about Same and Different by Linda Hayward

Same or Different by Barbara Gregorich

Keeping You Safe: A Book About Police Officers by Ann Owen

A Day with Police Officers by Jan Kottke

At the Beach by Mandy Stanley

Ribbons of Sand: Exploring Atlantic Beaches by Larry Points

CIRCLE TIME

Same/Different
(Show children two familiar items—a bathing suit and a coat, for example. Ask each child to tell a way the items are the same and a way they are different. Introduce new pairs of items as necessary until all children have had a turn.)

Vocabulary—Absurdities (Use after lesson 125.)
(Pick a new Common Information word such as thermometer. After going over the information rule *A thermometer is a tool for telling temperatures*, ask questions that require a yes or no answer about the word:)
Does a thermometer look at your eyes? *No.* That would be absurd!
Have you ever seen a thermometer? *Yes.*
Do you use a thermometer to eat with? *No.* That would be absurd!

Actions—Rules
(Play an Action rule game. Example:) "If the teacher says *do it,* stomp your feet." Let's see if I can fool you. (See if children can follow the rule. When children's responses are firm, ask a volunteer to make a rule for you and the rest of the group to follow.)

I Will Grow . . . . Predictable Chart—Classification
(Review with children the definition *If it grows in the ground, it is a plant.* Ask children to use their classification skills to think of things they could grow. On chart paper write **I will grow** _____. Then complete the sentence with the name of something that would grow. Give each child a turn to dictate a sentence as you write it on the chart. Put the child's name at the end of the sentence.
Note: This chart can be used in the Writing Center with the activity class book.)

TRANSITIONS

On the Move!

Months—Days
(You start saying the months of the year beginning with January and then point to a child. If the child can say the next month, he or she moves to next activity or lines up. Continue until all children have moved. Use this same activity with the days of the week.)

Let's Focus!

Where, Who, When, What
(Take pictures of your class doing various activities. Keep several of these pictures at hand. To refocus the group, hold up one of the photographs. Allow children a minute or two to study it. Then ask where, who, when, and what questions about the photo.)

CENTER ACTIVITIES

 *Art*

Painting—Locations: At the Farm

Provide a large piece of finger-paint paper for each child. Have children paint the bottom half of their sheets of paper brown and green for land and paint the top half blue for the sky. Allow paint to dry. Using red construction paper, have children trace around the barn-shaped cardboard tracer, cut out the barn, and glue it on the painted paper. Provide die cuts of farm animals to glue on their sheets of paper, or have children draw their own farm animals. Encourage children to share their farm paintings with the rest of the class. As children are working, ask them to say the whole thing about a farm. *A farm is a place where food is grown.*

 Dramatic Play

Seasons

Organize children in small groups, and assign each group a season—winter, spring, summer, fall. Group members act out things they might do in that season as the rest of the class tries to guess the activity and name the season. Examples: swimming/summer; snow skiing/winter; planting seeds/spring; and raking leaves/fall.

 Games

What's in the Bag?—Same/Different

For each pair of children, provide a paper bag and a collection of eight small objects that are alike in some ways and different in others. For example: two small stuffed animals might be the same size but different shapes. To play, each pair of children takes turns pulling two things out of the bag. The child compares the two objects and tells how they are the same or how they are different. Continue the game by letting children choose two other objects to compare.

 Games

Cover Up!—Opposites

Provide each child with a copy of BLM 120A and a copy of BLM 120B from Language Activity Masters Book 1, and follow the directions on page 62. Taking turns, children draw a card and talk about it and its opposite. The child then places the card on its opposite on the game board. The game continues until all spots on the game board are covered.

Materials: Finger-paint paper; green, brown, and blue paint; cardboard tracer of a barn; red construction paper; die cuts of farm animals (optional); scissors, glue

Materials: Pairs of objects such as a red block and a red toy car, a crayon and a marker, a glove and a mitten, a tennis ball and a golf ball

Materials: (see activity)

Materials:
Overhead
projector,
overhead
transparencies
(see activity)

☎ *Listening/Speaking*

Before/After

Photocopy and make overhead transparencies of the pictures from the following Before/After exercises in *Language for Learning* Presentation Book C: lesson 111, exercise 6; lesson 112, exercise 8; lesson 113, exercise 9; lesson 114, exercise 7; lesson 115, exercise 11. Cut the pictures apart. Working in pairs at the overhead, children put the pictures from each exercise in the correct sequence to tell the story. As children work, circulate and ask them questions following the Before/After format.

Materials:
Recording of
"Dozy Goes
Fishing,"
photocopies of
the story pictures,
drawing paper

☎ *Listening/Speaking*

Responding to a Story

Record the story "Dozy Goes Fishing" from Storybook 4. After children listen to the story, ask them what words Dozy does not know *(before* and *after)*. Photocopy the pictures from the story, and have children put the pictures in the correct sequence. Then ask children to draw a picture of something that happens in the story because Dozy does not know the words *before* or *after*. When children are finished, encourage them to share their pictures with the rest of the group.

Materials: Objects
made of paper,
objects made of
glass. Examples:
plates, drinking
glasses, bottles,
cups

🖩 *Math*

Sorting—Paper/Glass

Provide a variety of objects, some made of paper, some made of glass. Ask children to sort the objects by the type of material from which they are made. To extend the activity and prepare for future comparative exercises, provide a balance scale. Encourage children to put a glass object on the scale, then a paper object. Ask: Which is heavier? Which is lighter?

Materials: Large
blocks, matching
set of smaller
blocks

⚙ *Motor*

Blocks—Big/Small

Provide pairs of children with a pile of large blocks and a pile of small blocks. One child makes a simple building out of large blocks; the other child makes the identical building out of small blocks.

Materials: Ice,
2 bowls,
cold water,
thermometer
hot-water bottle

🧪 *Science*

Hot/Cold—Thermometers

Ask children to name things that are cold. Then ask them to name things that are hot. Put ice in one bowl. Ask children to predict whether ice is warm or cold. Invite each child to touch the ice to confirm the prediction. Set a hot-water bottle on the table. Ask children to predict whether the water bottle is warm or cold. Invite each child to touch the bottle to confirm the prediction. Pour cold water over the ice. Place a thermometer in the ice water, and tell children to watch the red line. Ask them to describe what happened to the red line. Pour water from the hot water bottle into an empty bowl, and put the thermometer in the water. Ask children to describe what happened to the red line.

✎ *Writing*

Class Book—I Will Grow

Materials: Drawing paper

Using the I Will Grow—Predictable Chart from the Circle Time activity, write each child's sentence at the bottom of a piece of drawing paper. Include each child's name, or have children write their own names if they are able. Read each child's sentence aloud, reminding the child what he or she planned to grow. Encourage children to draw pictures of their plants. Make a cover titled "Look at What We Are Growing," and staple all pages together, including an additional blank page, to create a class book. Type simple directions to family members asking them to write a sentence about what *they* would like to grow. Allow a different child to take the book home each night. As children bring the book back to school each morning, they share with the class what their family members would grow.

BOOKS FOR SHARED READING

Why Do Seasons Change: Questions Children Ask about Time and Seasons
    by Dorling Kindersley

Happy Face Sad Face by Lynn Offerman

On the Farm by Diane James

Farming by Gail Gibbons

Blue Sea by Robert Kalan

Here a Chick, There a Chick by Bruce McMillan

Who Uses This? by Margaret Miller

All Year Long by Nancy Tafuri

A Circle of Seasons by Myra Cohn Livingston

Mouse Days by Leo Lionni

CIRCLE TIME

Same/Different Scents
(Extend Same/Different with a scent-matching activity. For each child, make a response card with a smiling face on one side and a frowning face on the other. Cut three bottle shapes from construction paper. On each "bottle," rub a different fragrance such as cinnamon, orange extract, and cocoa powder. Next put a cinnamon stick, some orange wedges, and a chocolate bar in separate lunch bags. Pass one of the paper bottles for all children to smell. Next pass one of the lunch bags. Ask children to tell whether or not the scent in the bag is the *same* as the one on the bottle— hold up smiling face; or *different*—hold up frowning face.)

Occupations—Who Uses That?
(Collect items that relate to the occupations that have been taught—dentist, firefighter, teacher, carpenter, doctor, nurse, police officer, painter, pilot, lumberjack, librarian. Each day secretly place in a mystery box an item that relates to one of the occupations. Describe the item by giving one clue at a time. Children try to see how fast they can guess the name of the item and who uses it. Then have the children say the whole thing about this person.)

Seasons
(Show a picture of a different season each day at circle time. After the group has identified the season, ask individual children to name different activities that can be done during that season. For example: summer— swimming, going on vacation or to the beach, playing outside, and so on.)

TRANSITIONS

On the Move!

Names
(Pretend to be a photographer with an imaginary camera. Say: Smile for the camera. As you capture each child's attention, call out the child's name, and pretend to snap his or her picture. Once the picture has been taken, he or she can line up or move to the next activity.)

Let's Focus!

Actions
(Select a favorite song that has motions such as "I'm a Little Teapot." Whisper the words of the song while doing the motions, encouraging children to join in with you. Then repeat the song simply mouthing the words while doing the motions. All eyes will be on you.)

CENTER ACTIVITIES

Materials: Paint paper, paints

Art

Painting—Season

Invite children to paint a scene depicting the current season. Allow paint to dry. Then have children draw themselves in their scene doing a favorite seasonal activity. Ask children to tell you what they are doing and write or type their responses on a strip of paper. Example: *In the summer I like to go to the beach.* Glue the sentence strip to their painting. Make a cover titled "Summer" and staple all pages together to create a class book. Provide a page for family members' comments. Type simple directions to family members asking them to write their answer to the question "What do you like to do in (season)?" Allow different children to take the book home each night. As children bring the book back to school each morning, they share with the class what their family members wrote.

Materials: Props for a medical center, such as stethoscope, blood pressure cuff, forehead thermometers, masks, bandages

Dramatic Play

Medical Center

Change your Housekeeping Center to a Medical Center. Provide props such as a play stethoscope, a blood pressure cuff, and forehead thermometers. Encourage children to role-play doctor, nurse, and patient. Ask children to say the whole thing about a doctor, a nurse, and a patient.

Materials: *The Librarian from the Black Lagoon* by Mike Thaler, drawing paper

Listening

Responding to a Story

To reinforce *library* and *librarian* from the Common Information track, record the book *The Librarian from the Black Lagoon*. Provide drawing paper, and ask children to draw a picture of themselves in a library.

Materials: Pictures of "Dozy Goes on a Hike," hook-and-loop tape

Listening/Speaking

Story Retelling

Photocopy the pictures from "Dozy Goes on a Hike" from Storybook 4. Laminate the pictures, and attach a piece of hook-and-loop tape to the back of each. After children have heard the story read aloud several times, encourage them to attach the pictures to a flannel board as they retell the story in their own words.

Materials: For each child, one copy of BLM 125 from Language Activity Masters Book 1, crayons, scissors, one craft stick, glue

Listening/Speaking

Opposites

Make happy/sad puppets following directions on page 65 of Language Activity Masters Book 1. To vary the game, describe various situations where children may feel happy or sad. Have them give their response by showing the happy side of the puppet or the sad side. For example: Your friend got some new crayons and she shared them with you. How do you feel? Your baby brother tore the painting you brought home from school. How do you feel?

Math

Graphing Seasons

Using a large piece of freezer paper, divide it into four columns—one for each season—labeled with the word and a picture clue. For example: A clue for *fall* might be a picture of a tree losing its leaves. Have an assortment of die cuts available to represent each season. Examples: snowflake, daffodil, sunglasses, orange leaf. Ask children to choose a die cut that shows their favorite season. If they are able, have them write their names on it. Then have children glue their die cuts under the corresponding headings on the chart. After everyone has finished, discuss the graph with the class. Which season did children like the most? Which season did children like the least? Encourage individual children to tell why they picked their season.

Materials: Freezer paper, seasonal die-cut shapes, scissors, glue

Motor

Seasons

Use masking tape to make a large square on the floor. Divide the square into fourths. Label each fourth of the square with a picture and the name of one of the seasons. To play the game, one child sits in each square. The game begins with one child calling out the name of a season (not his or her own), and rolling a beach ball to the child sitting in the square labeled with that season. This child calls out another season, and rolls the ball to the child sitting in the corresponding square.

Materials: Masking tape, beach ball, pictures representing each season

Science

Same/Different Rocks

Put an assortment of rocks into a paper bag. Each child chooses two rocks from the bag. On a recording sheet, children draw rock 1 and rock 2. Then encourage each child to tell you how their rocks are the *same* and how they are *different*. Record their responses on their recording sheets for each rock. Invite children to share their rock drawings and findings with the class.

Materials: Paper bags, assortment of rocks

Sorting

Comparatives—Shorter/Taller

Collect empty paper towel, toilet paper, or wrapping paper tubes. Cut them in graduated heights, and cover them with colored paper. Encourage children to arrange the tubes in order from shortest to tallest. Then ask questions such as: Which tube(s) is (are) shorter than the red tube? Which tube(s) is (are) taller than the blue one?

Materials: Paper towel, toilet paper, or wrapping paper tubes; colored paper

Materials:
Postcards,
school names
and addresses
of other pre-k
or kindergarten
classes

Writing

Seasonal Pen Pals Postcard

Locate school names and addresses of pre-k or kindergarten classes where you can send postcards asking each class about their seasonal weather. This works particularly well if a class in the south sends a postcard to a class in the north or vice-versa. Help children dictate a list of questions to write on the postcards. For example: *What is your weather like today? How do you dress for winter? What are some games you play outside in winter?*

BOOKS FOR SHARED READING

The Librarian from the Black Lagoon by Mike Thaler

Circle of Seasons by Gerda Muller

The Very Small by Joyce Dunbar

Zoe's Hats: A Book of Colors and Patterns by Sharon Lane Holm

Look Book by Tana Hoban

Who's in the Shed? by Brenda Parkes

Who Sank the Boat? by Pamela Allen

Pancakes for Breakfast by Tomie DePaola

A House Is a House for Me by Mary Ann Hoberman

Barnyard Banter by Denise Fleming

CIRCLE TIME

Share Your News—Who, When, Where, What

(Ask for a volunteer to share some news with the class. Limit the news to one sentence. For example:) *Last night we went to the store.* (Next the volunteer asks:) *Are there any questions?* (The volunteer calls on classmates to ask questions about the news. The questions must begin with **who, when, where,** or **what.** Examples:) ***Who*** *did you go with?* ***What*** *store did you go to?*

I Spy—Materials

(Play the I spy game, but include the material the object is made of as one of the clues. The teacher or one of the children begins the game by giving clues that include such things as color or shape and then adds the type of material. For example: *I spy something that is red and made of plastic.* Play the game with the materials taught—plastic, wood, paper, concrete, metal, rubber, glass, cloth, leather.)

Information—Seasons

(Make four or more die-cut shapes to depict each season—snowflakes: winter, flowers: spring, orange leaves: fall, suns: summer. Arrange the shapes in a large circle, and tape them to the floor. In the center of the circle, place one seasonal item for each of the die-cut shapes. Some examples are a mitten, a flower, a toy rake, a sand bucket. To play, children stand in a circle. While music is played, they walk around the circle. When the music stops, children stop on one of the die cuts. You call out the name of a season. Each child who is standing on a die cut representing that season goes to the middle of the circle and chooses an object that represents that season. Children then return to their die cut with the item selected. The game continues until all four seasons have been called.)

Days of the Week

(Use rhythm sticks or clapping for this game. Start the game by saying:) Hey, Mr. Sunday, play a song for me. Hey, Mr. Sunday, play a song for me. (Clap or use the sticks in a simple rhythmic pattern. The children have to repeat the pattern. Continue the game with:) Hey, Mr. Monday, play a song for me. Hey, Mr. Monday, play a song for me. (Clap or use the sticks, repeating the same pattern or using a new one. The children repeat the pattern. Continue with each day of the week.)

TRANSITIONS

On the Move!

Seasons
(Laminate four pictures, each depicting a different season of the year. Tape these to the floor where children line up to leave the classroom. As children leave the room, each child names each season as he or she steps on the pictures.)

Let's Focus!

Cut two-inch squares from blue, red, yellow, green, orange, black, brown, and purple construction paper. Tape each square into a cylinder shape and slide the cylinders on your fingers. Using the tune to "Where Is Thumbkin?" sing this song whenever it is necessary to wait in line. Hold up a finger, and sing:) Where is **blue,** where is **blue?** Here I am, here I am. How are you this morning? Very well, I thank you. Fly away, fly away. (Continue with other colors. Children will focus on you to see what color is up next.)

CENTER ACTIVITIES

✂️ *Art*

Jungle—Culminating Activity

Culminate your year of language learning with a classroom-turned-jungle. Using green and brown bulletin board paper, twist long pieces into vine-like ropes, and loop them from the ceiling. Create a waterfall entrance to your classroom by attaching a five-feet-by-two-feet piece of clear plastic sheeting above your doorway. Cut the sheeting in three-inch wide strips from the bottom to the top. Have children make snakes from construction paper and add designs using brightly-colored markers. Hang the snakes from your vines. Provide brown construction-paper circles and rectangles. Have children put these together using paper fasterers to make monkeys. Add arms and tails, and hang the monkeys from the vines. Make parrots out of paper plates. Use a small one for the head and a large one for the body. Attach construction paper wings and beaks, and glue on some bright feathers. Add these to the vines. Finally, invite parents to come to your room, and have children serve pineapple upside-down cupcakes. (See Housekeeping Center activity.)

> **Materials:** Green and brown bulletin board paper, clear plastic sheeting, construction paper, markers, paper fasteners, large and small paper plates, glue, pineapple upside-down cupcake recipe

🖐️ *Dramatic Play*

Restaurant

Turn your Housekeeping Center into a restaurant. Put a tablecloth on a small table for customers. Provide props such as aprons for waiters, plates, cups, bowls, silverware, cash register, pretend money, pretend food, containers and wrappers from fast-food chains, menus from restaurants, and note pads and pencils for waiters to use to take orders. As children are playing, ask them to say the whole thing about a restaurant, a customer, and a waiter. *A restaurant is a place where you buy a meal. A customer is a person who buys something. A waiter is a person who brings your food in a restaurant.*

> **Materials:** Items found in a restaurant (see activity)

🖐️ *Dramatic Play*

Story Retelling

Make story pieces to go with "The Little Blue Bug." You will need to make a flowering plant with spotted leaves, several blue bugs, and one spotted bug. Laminate the pieces, and attach hook-and-loop tape on the back. Encourage children to retell the story "The Little Blue Bug" as they attach the pieces on the flannel board.

> **Materials:** Story pieces for "The Little Blue Bug," hook-and-loop tape, flannel board

🎲 *Games*

Classification

Make a game board. On each space glue a picture from the Classification track— vehicles, food, containers, clothing, animals, buildings, plant, tools, furniture. Children roll a number cube and move a marker the number of spaces shown. To

> **Materials:** Poster board, pictures from Classification track, number cube, game markers

play the game they must tell the classification of the picture they landed on. As children's responses become firm, the game can be extended to telling the class of the picture they land on (food, for example) and naming another object in that class (carrots, for example).

Games
Occupations and Related Objects
Prepare one copy of BLM 140A, and one copy of BLM 140B from Language Activity Masters Book 1, page 73. Either photocopy these on card stock or glue them to card stock and cut out the cards. Before playing, show children the cards, and ask them to identify the occupations and the tools. Children play this concentration-style game, making matches between the people and the tools they need for their jobs. The child must say the whole thing about the pictures: *This is a farmer. This is a tractor.* For complete directions, see Language Activity Masters Book 1, page 73.

Housekeeping
Cooking—Sequencing: Pineapple Upside-Down Cupcake
Ingredients for one pineapple upside-down cupcake are:
1 teaspoon brown sugar
1 teaspoon crushed pineapple
1/4 cup yellow cake batter.
(See cake mix box for additional ingredients and baking time and temperature.)
Provide rebus recipe cards with drawings that show the following four steps in sequence to make a pineapple upside-down cupcake: 1) 1 teaspoon brown sugar placed in a foil cupcake liner; 2) 1 teaspoon crushed pineapple added; 3) 1/4 cup of cake batter added; 4) put cupcake liners in cupcake tin and bake in the oven. Arrange the ingredients near the step-by-step direction cards. Cool cupcakes, and turn upside down to eat.

Listening/Speaking
Responding to a Story
Record a reading of "Miss Edna Does the Same Thing" from Storybook 4. Photocopy the story pictures for children to look at while they listen to the story. After they listen to the story, ask children to draw a picture of something they like to do that is always the *same* every day. Then ask children to draw a picture of something they like to do that is *different* because they don't get to do it every day. Encourage children to tell about their *same* and *different* pictures.

Fine Motor

Drawing—Part/Whole

Cut out pictures from magazines showing objects taught in the Part/Whole exercises—wagon, toothbrush, flower, tree, umbrella, coat, broom, cabinet, elephant. Cut off a part from each object. For example, cut a wheel from the wagon, the handle from the toothbrush, and the stem from a flower. Laminate the pictures, and provide children with dry-erase markers. Encourage children to look at the pictures and to figure out what part is missing. They can then draw the missing part using the marker.

Sorting

Materials

Provide several objects made from the materials children have learned—wood, paper, concrete, metal, rubber, glass, plastic, cloth, leather. Place these objects on a tabletop. Encourage children to sort the objects according to the material from which they are made. Ask children to explain their sorts when they are finished.

Writing

Flip Book—Seasons

Draw a simple tree trunk with bare branches on a quarter-sheet of paper (winter). Make three additional simple treetop drawings on an eighth-sheet of paper. Show one treetop with some small leaves and flowers (spring); show another treetop with some leaves attached and some falling (fall), and show a third treetop with full, bushy leaves (summer). Make photocopies for each child. Direct children to color the treetops appropriately to depict the four seasons. Then staple the treetops over the quarter-sheet tree (winter) to form a flip-book showing spring, summer, fall, and winter.

Note: For an additional flip-book activity, see Language Activity Masters Book 1, page 76, showing absurdities with jungle animals.

Materials:
Laminated pictures of objects taught in Part/Whole exercises, dry-erase markers

Materials: Objects made of materials learned in lessons

Materials: Seasons drawings described in activity, crayons, stapler

BOOKS FOR SHARED READING

Walking through the Jungle by Julie Lacome

Jungle Animals by Angela Royston

Touch and Feel Jungle Animals by Nicola Deschamps

Little Penguin by Patrick Benson

Sitting in My Box by Dee Lillegard

To Bathe a Boa by Imbior Kudrna

Benny Bakes a Cake by Eve Rice

The Day Jimmy's Boa Ate the Wash by Trinka Hakes Noble

Somebody and the Three Blairs by Marilyn Tolhurst

Who Can Boo the Loudest? by Harriet Ziefert